Ways To Overcome Financial Disasters in One's Life

By

Malcolm Coneo

Preface

The main purpose for writing this book is to educate the masses on ways to improve one's finances. In modern societies kids are taught math, science, reading, history, but not finances. Although the core courses are important, I believe financial literacy is an integral part in forming a young student's overall education. For example, in our current education system, kids are not taught about basic finances such as the importance of life insurance, bitcoin, how to finance one's post-secondary education, and other topics.

To educate people on basic financing I will be utilizing small common everyday stories to drill key concepts. Hopefully when the book has been read the information can be helpful to anyone interested in learning basic financial topics. Enjoy!

Chapter 1

Introduction

In this modern age filled with cell phones, social media, bills, work, school, and family life can be quite stressful. Having too much stress can be bad for one's health. Some of the ailments of too much stress are fatigue, anxiety, depression, angry outbursts, social withdrawal, that eventually lead to heart problems, high blood pressure, and diabetes. Although too much stress is bad for one's health, a little stress can be quite good.

For example, stress within normal levels can help all of us become better workers, entrepreneurs, artists, students, spouses, and friends. If there was no stress in the world, everything would stand still and progress slowly! Therefore, all of us need some healthy stress in our lives.

A major stressor for most people is personal finances. People dread talking about finances. Countless studies conducted over the years have consistently placed finances as top of the problem for many families globally. To deal with finances, one must confront the situation directly! By postponing finances, one only gets into a deeper hole! Almost everything in our daily lives revolves around finances. All of us pay for groceries, gas, rent, mortgages, taxes, car notes, credit cards, insurance and of course funeral costs! Also finances play an integral part in our personal and business relationships. For example, a large percentage of divorces are due to financial difficulties amongst couples. Therefore, it is imperative for people to take finance as a serious matter.

Finances are not that difficult. Anybody who can do arithmetic and is disciplined with his or her finances can be financially healthy! If one has been struggling with finances in the past, you have come to the right place.

Chapter 2

Real Estate

For most people, the biggest investment in one's life is the purchase of a home. When a residence is purchased, one feels a sense of independence, confidence, and accomplishment. The smell of a new home can be quite intoxicating and seductive for a new homeowner.

However, when one buys a home a variety of costs is involved. One must pay mortgage payments, utility bills, property taxes, landscaping, and home insurance. Pretty soon the beautiful and pristine house can quickly turn into a nightmare! In the following example, a fellow named Mark can attest to the fact that a dream home can be a nightmare when costs are not considered.

Hello, my name is Mark. I was born in the beautiful, exciting, and tropical paradise of Miami, Florida. Since I was a young man, I loved working with my hands. My goal was to finish high school and start working in a trade profession. Fortunately, before I graduated from high school I fell in love with electrical work.

Immediately after graduating from high school, I went straight to work as a journeyman electrician for a construction company. Three years later I became a licensed electrician and went into business for myself. I married my high school sweetheart Anna, which is the love of my life and had two boys. Also, during this time Anna completed her drafting certificate at a local community college with top honors and started working at an engineering firm. During the next eight years my electrical business flourished.

As the years passed swiftly, my wife and I decided to buy a bigger house for our family. The house my wife and I decided to purchase was a Mediterranean style residence that is about five thousand square feet living area. Our gorgeous residence consists of five bedrooms, two bathrooms, a large living room used as an entertainment center, and a kitchen which has beautiful marble countertops and cedar oak cabinets!

The house also has a beautiful and large backyard consisting of a nicely decorated pool surrounded by smooth natural rocks, a wooden gazebo made of fresh cedar that is to die for! Family and friends loved the gazebo which is large enough to enjoy dancing, good conversation, and drinks during evening times. Due to having a large backyard Anna planted a fruit garden that grows plums, peaches, oranges, and apples.

Anna and I bought the house in 2003. The first four years were a blast. Nothing but happiness and joy filled our house. For my family and I it seemed we were all living in the enchanted kingdom of Camelot! At the time, it seemed like good times would last forever!

Everything was about to change! One of my friends was telling me he knew a couple of people who had their homes foreclosed due to an unexpected rise in interest rates on their mortgages. For example, instead of paying seven hundred dollars a month on his or her mortgage the monthly payment jumped to one thousand three hundred dollars! In retrospect, I thought the people who had their homes foreclosed were irresponsible and undisciplined! Man, I was wrong by a long shot! I could not fathom the catastrophe that would befall the real estate industry, but also my entire life!

As 2007 ended the so-called foreclosure crisis started to heat up considerably! I was still positive the situation was going to improve due to my happy go lucky attitude. However, as days turned into weeks and weeks into months, the housing crisis got worse. By June of 2008 it was getting very ugly. It seemed the Miami real estate market was falling apart at a rapid rate! Reality was hitting me and my friends very hard!

My contracts started to slow dramatically. When I used to have work for months in advance, I was getting contracted for just three jobs a week, which forced me to cut workers! At first, I tried to cut hours, but as the recession progressed and got worse, I had no other choice. By the end of 2009 it was horrible. That year was probably the worst year of my entire life!

Adding salt to injury I was falling behind on my mortgage payment. Like many of my neighbors in Miami and fellow Americans across the great country of the United States interest rates were increasing, which made it difficult and even impossible to keep up with mortgage payments. In addition, the value of homes dropped substantially during 2008. Millions of homes   declined in value thirty to forty percent, including my residence!

By early 2010 I was doing all the work for my company. My wife was also hustling two jobs to help pay the mortgage and maintain the house. Anna and I were struggling with the mortgage payments and other expenses. On an early Saturday morning, around six before Dawn was to appear, my wife and I were sitting outside enjoying a wonderful breakfast she had made, which was quite delicious. The breakfast consisted of scrambled eggs, wheat toast, bacon, fruit, and coffee. The boys were asleep at the time.

My wife and I started to talk about the good old times and work. Both of us had been so busy trying to get money anyway possible that we rarely spoke to one another. Anna told me bluntly that we were just killing ourselves, so the best thing to do is give up the house. Anna's had always loved the house since its inception. To her the house was like her fairy tale castle she had dreamed of as a little girl. My lovely wife emphasized that everything will be fine if the family works together as a team.

Four months later Anna, the kids, and I lost the home to foreclosure. During those four months we sold most of our material possessions. In the meantime, Anna had been in constant contact with her cousin Janie. Fortunately, Janie and Anna had always been close since they were little girls. Both were in the girl scout troupe and members of the church choir for many years. Janie and her husband Peter were born and raised in Miami, like Anna and me. However, fifteen years ago Janie and Peter moved to Houston, Texas because Peter had found a new job as a project engineer for a large global oil conglomerate.

Although Peter and Janie had gone to Houston, we always kept in touch with one another. Anytime Peter and Janie would come to Miami we would go with them to Disney World and other places across Florida, especially beautiful Destin! Janie and Anna would call each other every week talking about their lives and comforting one another.

As soon as Gregory started his job in Houston Janie had an idea to commence a catering business. Ever since Janie was a young girl she loved to cook. Cooking for her was not work, but an intense passion! I mean the woman cooks delicious. With the encouragement of her husband, she started small and had a few clients at first. However, with patience, dedication, and hard work Janie's catering business has grown tremendously and employs forty people. Janie can hustle!

In just fifteen years Janie and Peter paid off their home in a nice suburb in Houston with good schools for their kids and all the modern conveniences. The only thing Janie and Peter complained about was the beaches of Galveston were nothing like the pristine beaches of Miami!

Janie had heard all over the news that the real estate market in Miami had been collapsing dramatically. It was like the city reached a standstill! Anna had told Janie the real estate situation was terrible. All I know is one conversation led to another, and Janie convinced my wife and I it was probably time to come to Houston. Although the country was facing a recession at the time Houston and Texas in general were relatively unscathed. To tell you the truth my wife and I were a little apprehensive at first. However, Anna and I came to the realization we had to do what was best for the family. The kids were sad we were leaving Miami but accepted the decision.

My wife, kids, and I left Miami during the summer, so the kids could complete their school year. A week later after the kids had finished, we packed our stuff in a U-Haul and around six in the morning left Miami and ventured towards Houston. I told my family we were embarking on a new adventure in our lives.

Thanks to the help of Peter and Janie, Anna and I found an affordable house to rent in a neighborhood with good schools for the kids. A month after our family settled in Houston, to my surprise I was working with an electrical company which has great benefits and pay. In the weekends I would do private electrical contract work to supplement my income, so I would have more money to invest! Anna found a job as a drafter for a large natural gas company based in Houston with great benefits due to her extensive experience. Slowly, but surely our family was pulling up from the economic abyss. When the kids started school in Texas, I was surprised both boys adjusted well.

Six years later my wife and I had saved enough money to buy a new house for a reasonable price. The house my wife and I bought was much smaller than the previous one in Miami. Also, my wife and I got a low fixed interest rate for twenty years. The house was smaller, but it required less maintenance, and lower expenses! By lowering our household costs the money can be used for retirement and travel! To tell you the truth we are much stronger and happier as a family after going through the horrible ordeal of losing our home. My wife and I learned from the so called "housing bust" is one does not need a big house to be happy, but a strong stable family and friends who will be with you during good and bad times!

Sincerely,

Mark Houston Texas USA

Now Mark that was a nice and inspirational story. Although Mark and his family suffered through their ordeal, the family corrected their mistakes and went on with their lives. Mark and Anna realized having a humongous house can be quite a headache!

In the next story a female named Louisa will share a story about her real estate experience.

Hello, my name is Louisa. I was born in Wilmington, Delaware some years back. A year after my birth mom passed away unexpectedly. I do not remember her, but relatives and my father told me mom was crazy about me. Fortunately, I have a wonderful father and grandmother who raised me in a loving and stable environment. The first two years of schooling, I struggled academically, which led to me being held back one year. However, my dad was patient and constantly working with me on improving my grades. As soon as dad came from work, he would help me do my homework and made sure I read daily.

With persistence, patience, and encouragement from my father and grandmother my grades steadily improved. In a couple of years, I became academically proficient which enabled me to skip a couple of grades. By eighth grade I was reading at college level!

Throughout my high school years, I made friends and dated a few of my classmates. I was actively involved with the math and science club, drama, long distance running, and my favorite activity orchestra! Since I first heard classical music, I fell in love with the violin. My dad started me in private lessons at the age of seven years old. Over time I developed into a good violinist. At the age of sixteen during my junior year I won a violin contest in the city of Wilmington and had the honor of performing in New York City with other young musicians from Delaware. By going to New York City, it helped expand my intellectual horizons where I met other bright young musical students from across the country. I also went on a visit to the prestigious Julliard School for performing arts and met faculty and students who were friendly.

The trip to New York inspired me to study more and work on my craft. As the seasons came and went, I graduated from high school with top honors and was the valedictorian of the graduating class of five hundred students. The most important moment for me was when my grandmother and dad were part of the audience. When I gave the speech at the graduation commencement, I made sure to thank my family. My grandmother and father could have given up on me so long ago, but they stayed the course! A week after graduating from high school, Wellesley admissions informed me via mail correspondence that I had been accepted to attend in the fall. My grandmother and father kissed and hugged me so hard. I was just so jubilant!

Three months passed, and my dad and grandma helped me unpack the dorm room where I was going to live for the next four years. As I opened the door my face came into direct contact with the person, I was going to share the room for the next four years, Allison Gonzalez from New York City. Unbeknownst to me at the time was that Allison and I would be lifelong and best friends. Allison introduced herself to my father, grandmother and me. I could tell at first glance Allison is a people person and possesses a cheerful demeanor.

As the four years passed in the blink of an eye, I had many highs and lows along my journey as a student. At times I would feel overwhelmed by university life but remained steadfast on my educational experience thanks to countless friends, professors, and Allision. Allison graduated with a degree in chemistry with high honors.   I finished with a double major in Math and Music with honors. I was excited and ready to tackle the future with confidence!! Allison and I were blessed we had jobs after graduation in downtown Boston.

Dad wanted to reward me for graduating from college with a vacation to beautiful Cancun with its enchanting beaches. Although my grandmother and father were older at the time both were still healthy due to their lifestyle of eating healthy and exercise. The two weeks in Mexico was a beautiful adventure for the three of us. We toured the surrounding areas which were filled with beautiful ecosystems and buildings built by the Mayas. Returning from vacation I was energized and ready to work. On the first day of my new job, I was a little nervous, but excited to start my career! When five years has passed rapidly, dad had remarried to a beautiful and well-educated high school English teacher. I strongly believe dad picked the right woman to grow old with. My grandmother was doing well health wise, and her mental skills were still sharp!

At this time, I was promoted to lead the trading division in New York City. However, before I relocated to New York City, I had to sell the townhome! Fortunately, the townhouse was sold for a nice profit.

Arriving in New York City I rented a nice and beautiful apartment on the seventh floor with two beautiful bedrooms, one bathroom, kitchen, and a living room. The apartment is about one thousand two hundred square feet in size, which is comfortable and easy to maintain. I have a little Dachshund named Phil who keeps me company and protects my home.

The next four years were quite stressful but my team and me were rewarded handsomely. Due to being compensated well I invested in eight houses in Florida. My goal was to rent the properties for a couple of years and then sell them at a nice profit! Unfortunately, I learned quickly the past does not guarantee future success in real estate. A few months before the Great Recession was about to commence, I was noticing defaults were rising steadily in the mortgage market. As I delved deeper into the data, I had an eerie feeling something nasty was going to take the American economy down!

When three months had passed my initial inclination that the economic situation would end badly came to fruition. Millions of people in the United States and across the world were let go from their jobs. At the time it seemed the entire financial system was about to collapse! Thankfully the financial system did not collapse because it would have caused more economic, social, and psychological damage!! I remember like it happened a second ago, all the employees around lunch time were summoned to a meeting. The event was out of place because we always had meetings early in the morning or late afternoon. Looking back my female intuition told me something bad was about to happen! For the first few minutes the president of the company was saying how great are the employees of the company. Next, he came with the bombshell the company was bleeding money. Finally, the president informed everyone in the conference room that each of us would have a job for two more weeks!

Many of my colleagues were shocked and others cried. I tried my best to console my colleagues. I personally felt crestfallen and betrayed! Two weeks elapsed rather rapidly, and I was unemployed! During the two weeks I was thinking about what I was going to do with my life and how to cover my expenses. Fortunately, I had plenty of savings for at least a year. I was grateful I had listened to my dad and grandmother regarding saving for a rainy-day fund if something unexpected was to occur!!

In the coming months things went from bad to utterly depressing! The houses I had bought and planned to flip in Miami for a decent profit had been lost. I had tried desperately to keep the residences, but I was unable to find buyers! It seemed buyers were running from houses like vampires from the cross!! During this time, I was extremely stressed and was unable to sleep due to the incessant worry of how I was going to unload the properties. On a cold rainy Saturday night around ten in the evening I was enjoying a delicious hot chocolate and just contemplating my situation. I decided to declare bankruptcy! Why fight a losing battle which was causing me spiritual, physical and mental anguish! Therefore, I decided to proceed with bankruptcy without any regret!!!

Fortunately, I had set up my real estate investments as a limited liability corporation so I could protect my pension, vehicle, and other investments. The next two weeks I set up the paperwork for bankruptcy filings. Although I knew my credit would be annihilated, I felt like I had melted tons of loan obligations off my back!

As time passed, I consolidated my debts and moved forward with my life. Luckily my small family, best friend Allison, and little dog helped me throughout my rough ordeal! Over the next couple of years, the economy improved slowly. I decided to downsize and leave New York City. New York had lost its luster and its magic on my soul, so I returned home to Delaware.

In the next couple of years, I started a company, which was always a dream of mine. I got the funds from side hustles such as running a weekend podcast on basic financial investing for regular people, and I had written two mystery novels. I saved up my money and went all in with the business. Dad, stepmom, grandmother, and close friends supported and inspired my dream. My niche market was helping companies deal with bankruptcies. I managed to get long term contracts with many companies after working seven days a week for consecutive months. Sometimes to progress one literally must work like one is insane!!!

I hired eighteen employees, and the business was quite successful. In my wildest dreams I would have never imagined making more money in Wilmington than New York City! I also felt much happier and enjoyed the tranquility of a slower paced lifestyle which enabled my family and I to travel across Europe and Asia. To see my family, enjoy the trips with their beautiful smiles, made my soul feel a sense of calm, joy, and inner peace!

With some of the profits made from my business, I managed to purchase a small rundown apartment complex at a good price. In a couple of months, I had occupants living in the renovated apartment complex. This time I viewed real estate as a long-term investment, instead of a short term get rich thing occupation. Looking back, I learned a lot about myself as a person. I could have easily broken apart, but I just kept going and knew all tempests must end one day and the radiant sun would eventually appear! Love you all people! From Wilmington, with love!

Thanks so much Louisa for your heart warming and inspiring story. The next story pertains to an older couple who are from the beautiful city of Seattle, Washington.

Hello, my name is Edward Caggiano. I was born and raised in Seattle, Washington. My parents were originally from New York, but ended up in Seattle because Boeing was hiring lots of people after World War two! Dad and mom left New York hell bent on seeking their fortune. My dad was twenty-four and mother twenty-two at the time. God bless their souls! A week passed and father started working at Boeing. Dad would eventually retire from Boeing after forty-two years of service with a great pension. Two weeks after dad got employed, mom started working for the US postal service. During the next five years mom and dad managed to save enough money to purchase a house. A year after my parents purchased the house, my older sister was born and about a year later, I came into existence. My sister and I are part of the baby boomer generation which would fuel the so-called consumer spending culture as we got older. I have to say my childhood years were fun, comfortable, and filled with unforgettable beautiful memories! One example was every summer the whole family would go to Acapulco, Mexico. Back in the days Acapulco was the place to go for many Americans and elite Hollywood stars because of its beautiful beaches, family activities, delicious food, and safety.

I completed my high school education with high honors. My main passions in high school were robotics and science. Since I was a young kid, I always loved math and science and knew early in life my goal was eventually to become an engineer! My dad and mom encouraged my sister and I to be whatever we wanted! Due to finishing in the top 10 of my graduating high school class I earned a full ride scholarship to the University of Washington. Back then education was much more affordable than today. By God I feel sorry for these kids who must pay so much for an education!

The next four years passed swiftly, and I graduated with a degree in Aeronautical engineering. My sister also graduated from the University of Washington, but a year earlier. Both parents were very proud of our accomplishments. I took a month off after graduation to relax a bit and prepare for the start of my engineering career. About a week before my month-long vacation was to end, I received a call from Boeing informing me I would join the company. As a young inexperienced, twenty-two-year-old kid, I felt on top of the world! Youth!!

Forty-five years after I graduated from college a lot had transpired. My loving father and mother had passed away. Four years after dad retired from Boeing, he developed brain cancer and died a year later. Life can be cruel and unfair! Mother enjoyed more of her retirement, but unfortunately, while going on a trip with her sister to beautiful Cabo had a massive stroke in the hotel suite. Horrible ending for such a loving and beautiful soul!

Well, on the positive side I have a wonderful and supporting wife and three boys to help me get through life's ups and downs. I managed to acquire a large house when Seattle was affordable and paid off the mortgage a couple of years before retiring from Boeing. The house that I worked hard for is about four thousand square feet living area with five rooms, living room, kitchen, study and 2 ½ bathrooms, with a large backyard and swimming pool. To my wife and I our home is not a location, but a place where many memories have taken place over the years. By this time the three boys had left the house and moved out of the state seeking financial opportunities.

A couple of years after retiring my wife and I had a long conversation about downsizing. Although we loved the house immensely due to the many beautiful experiences, it was becoming difficult to maintain. Therefore, we decided it was time to downsize into a smaller residence. Getting old sucks! Two of the boys had moved to Dallas, Texas where they had jobs in the high paying energy sector and my other son lives in lovely Austin where he makes lots of money in the technology market!   So, my wife and I decided emphatically Texas was the place for us to retire. My wife and I placed our beloved house for sale. To our astonishment the house was sold in just two weeks! Thank God we cashed out before a market crash!! Trust me, I have seen a few in my lifetime!

With the proceeds my wife and I were able to pay for a new home in a nice quiet suburb outside Dallas that would be close to the kids. All three sons were excited and understood their parents had made a wise choice to downsize. The house we purchased was much smaller than our previous household, but my wife and I were so happy because it was quick and easy to clean. I love our new neighborhood amenities such as a magnificent golf course and lovely nature trails. A large percentage of our neighbors are baby boomers from California and New York who relocated to Texas for its lower housing costs! The only thing I hate about Texas is the humidity!!! Nothing like cool crisp Seattle, with its beautiful mountains and evergreen forests where I used to hike with my parents, kids, and wife not too long ago!! Well with a smaller house and diminished maintenance costs, my wife and I have more flexibility with our money and are better able to travel across the country with ease. Overall, I am blessed to have a loving and supporting family. Happy to be an adopted Texan. Yawl take care. Even adopting a Texan accent!!

Real Estate Concepts to Remember

1. For most of the time real estate tends to appreciate over time. However, in some difficult economic situations like the Great Depression (1929- 1933) and Great Recession (2007- 2009) real estate prices can drop dramatically!

2. When one purchases a residence, many things must be considered! Costs that need to be considered are mortgage payments, home

insurance, property taxes, maintenance, security, and utilities!

3. Try to make sure that a residence meets one's budget. Each buyer of a residence has a different economic situation. Remember at the end of the day, the mortgage loan is under one's name, not anyone else!

4. Shop around lending institutions such as banks and credit unions to find the best rates. These days it is super easy to find rates via smart phones and other electronic devices. Also make sure the rates remain the same for the duration of the loan!

5. If one wants to buy real estate as
    an investment educate oneself as
    much as possible!! Start small
    and learn from seasoned
    investors. Remember the United
    States was not built in one day!
    Do not be afraid to ask questions.
    Learn one's local market first!
    Stay persistent.

Chapter 3

Automobiles

For most people having an automobile is an essential part in one's life. Most of us need automobile transportation to get to our jobs, school, buy groceries, social functions, and other daily activities. These days everything is so far away that not having an automobile can be a problem! The next couple of stories will include perspectives of buying an automobile.

Hello, my name is Thomas. I am from the beautiful state of California. About eight years ago I was promoted to a supervisory position at a manufacturing plant. I was so ecstatic about being promoted that I decided to reward myself by purchasing a new vehicle. All I wanted at the time was a custom Cadillac Escalade with a silver color, nice rims, leather seats, and a great sound system! I found my dream car just eight miles from my residence.

I called Monday morning so I could set up an appointment after work with a salesman. Even though I was focused on my work, I was constantly thinking of buying a Cadillac Escalade. The minutes felt like hours and hours like days. When it was five o'clock, I got in my car and went directly to the dealership. The next day I brought my new Escalade to work. Man, that was a great feeling!

I felt like I was flying above the pristine white clouds of the crystal-clear blue sky. My coworkers were surprised at my new car. I could see their jealousy in their eyes, and I loved teasing them, which brought me much excitement and delight! For the next three years I enjoyed and loved my Cadillac Escalade. I would take my many girlfriends on weekends to enjoy the California weather, hiking trails, and dance clubs. However, one Friday morning a couple of weeks before Christmas, management announced bluntly the manufacturing center where I worked was to close immediately due to intense competition from China.

Man, I was caught with my pants down! My coworkers and I were angry because all of us invested a large part of our lives for the company! All of us felt deeply underappreciated. That Christmas and New Years was quite depressing!

I thought I would find a quick job due to my experience and impeccable credentials. Months passed and no luck finding a job. In the meantime, bills were piling up and my car note was becoming difficult to pay. All I can say is high interest rates can kill a person! Now I was beginning to regret not reading the fine print. A couple of months later I had to let my baby go! I had to decide either food and rent or keep paying my expensive car loan. Some months passed and I finally managed to land a good job because one of my friends knew the hiring manager of the company.

My friend strongly recommended me to the position. All I can say is networking makes life easier for everyone involved. For the next ten months I would wake up early in the morning and catch a bus to work. As the months passed rapidly, I wanted to buy a car, but this time I would study my car purchase more carefully. I had made a humongous mistake when I purchased the Cadillac Escalade. This time I looked at a variety of vehicles, price and financing requirements. By carefully doing my homework I ended up getting a less expensive vehicle, but one that is of high quality.

Thanks Thomas from California.

Here is another story about purchasing an automobile.

Hello, I hope everyone had a wonderful and glorious morning. My name is Jennifer, and I am from Portland, Oregon. I graduated from UCLA with a degree in finance and a minor in mathematics. Go Bruins!! After graduating from UCLA, I went to work for the Peace Corps in Colombia. I spent two years in Colombia and worked as an English instructor and logistics coordinator for the corps. I fell in love with the food, culture, people, and majestic scenery.

Colombia's verdant mountains that reach the clouds, which resembled the color of winter snow, captivated my imagination. The beaches of Colombia are spectacular filled with crystal clear water with a turquoise color and white sand the color of precious pearls. During my stay in Colombia, I improved my Spanish tremendously. When the two years were completed with the Corps, I landed a job as a financial adviser in Phoenix, Arizona. For the next couple of months, I studied diligently for the series 7 and 66 so I could sell investments.

After passing the Securities examinations, I wanted to reward myself for the hard work and effort with a new vehicle. I had been using public transportation to get around for some time. I wanted a red BMW land shark like the color of a precious red ruby.   When I had attained the lowest interest rate on my loan, I finally chose a dealership. I haggled with the salespeople till I got a good deal. I want all to know haggling can be intimidating but in the long term will save people a lot of money and financial distress down the road! Thankfully, my dad taught me to bargain at an early age, but anyone can learn to haggle with practice! A week later I drove out in my beautiful BMW and felt on top of the world!

The only problem was the car would depreciate quickly in value and maintenance would be expensive. Fortunately, I did not have to drive far to work. My work is just ten minutes away which helps delay maintenance costs and depreciation. I use mass transit or Uber on weekends to go to museums, theater, and dance clubs with friends. I just found a balance and am doing well. Sincerely, Jennifer

from beautiful Phoenix.

These two stories are quite compelling. The stories cover important aspects of purchasing a vehicle.

These are points to remember when purchasing a vehicle that will cause less stress and pain in the future.

1. When looking for a vehicle, decide what one can afford. Always try to keep within budget.

2. When looking for a car loan look at various financial institutions. Always shop around for a low interest rate that can save thousands of dollars in loan repayments in the future. Come prepared with an approved loan before entering a dealership!

3. Once a loan has been approved go to three or four dealerships. Do not be afraid to shop around for great offers. Remember at the end of the day it's your hard-earned money!

No one else is responsible, but oneself for the loan!!

4. Remember that once a vehicle leaves a dealership it starts to depreciate. Sometimes up to 20 %!!! Always keep that in mind!

5. Maintenance and insurance costs are part of owning a vehicle. Therefore, choose a vehicle that is within one's budget.

6. Always try to imagine if one was terminated from a job would he or she be able to afford a car note payment for the next three months. Sometimes finding a good job can take some time to find, especially these days!!

Chapter 4

Education

For many people the second biggest financial investment after a house is an education. Many families across the entire planet are aware that a good quality education helps determine social mobility and financial prosperity. However, in the last fifteen years education has become extremely expensive.

When I was attending a state college in Texas a course with books would cost about four hundred fifty dollars on average, which was less than eighteen years ago. Now the same course presently costs about one thousand seven hundred fifty dollars! This means a full course load of twelve credit hours would cost more than seven thousand dollars without books. Keep in mind room, utilities, laundry, and food are not included. Imagine a private university tuition cost! Even with 529 education plans in many instances, might not be enough to cover education costs.

In the next few paragraphs, a couple of people will share their educational experiences. Enjoy the read!

Hi, my name is Juliana. Right now, I am thirty-four years old and currently work as a data scientist. About two years ago I managed to find a beautiful place to rent because my economic situation had significantly improved. Previously I had been living with my parents due to a difficult job market and expensive student loans. In the following paragraphs I will share my student loan experience.

I graduated as the valedictorian of my class which enabled me to acquire scholarship money. However, unbeknownst to me at the time the private liberal arts university I attended turned out to be quite expensive. The scholarships I had attained covered only about sixty percent of tuition, which did not include food and board. To pay for the rest of my education I needed to apply for student loans.

After changing majors, a couple of times, I graduated with a degree in theater. I loved the college experience and met a lot of cool people. However, the only thing I did not like at all was the debt I accrued!!!! Horrible!! The student loan amount ended up costing me about sixty-five thousand dollars! Yikes!

I was fortunate to find a job as a business consultant in California in 2003 due to an internship with the company. I learned very early one must establish good connections to get a decent job in this new economy!

My main objective was to pay my loan as soon as I started producing some income. I moved to magnificent, San Diego, California and was fortunate enough to rent an apartment just fifteen minutes away from my job! During the next few years, I threw my entire soul into the job that enabled me to travel all over the United States rebuilding businesses from the ground up! In addition, I had great benefits and a good income.

That was so cool, yet so long ago. In 2007 we received hefty bonuses that were so out of sight!! My career seemed bright with limitless opportunity. However, the so-called Great Recession had to show its ugly head. Close to the end of 2008 the consulting firm who I worked for was getting fewer contracts because companies were cutting budgets like crazy! It seemed people were being let go from their jobs in all directions.

One day in the morning one of my managers said we had an urgent meeting. Ten minutes into the meeting management told us the company was facing difficult challenges and regrettably drastic changes had to be made. Many of my fellow employees and I were given pink slips. Management gave us three weeks to work. My reaction to the announcement was complete shock!

Three weeks passed quickly, and I was out of a job. The next year and a half were total hell!! I had many interviews, but no job offers. In retrospect the interviews were a waste of time. At times I would find small consulting gigs but would not be enough to pay my mounting bills. In 2010 my financial situation became unbearable that I had to swallow my pride and go back home to Cleveland, Ohio. It was a tough decision.

I felt like a complete loser, but fortunately my mom and dad were supportive. I managed to find a full-time job as a barista for an independent coffee shop and felt a sense of purpose I had lacked for a long time. For about two years I did my job with great passion and enthusiasm.

One day out of the blue I started to talk to one of the regular customers in detail. The young man whose name is Paul informed me he had started a pharmaceutical company and needed people with managerial experience and tech savvy.

I told Paul about my experience as a business consultant. Paul was captivated by my experience that he scheduled a follow up interview in a couple of weeks. Finally, the day of the interview came and went. All I knew was I had tried my best!

Three weeks later I was working in a new startup and getting paid much better than my first job with good benefits. As time passed the company kept on growing and my financial position started to improve as well. I also refinanced my loan to a lower interest rate which made it easier to pay back my student loans. In five years, I managed to pay back my loan, which was a great relief!

Now that I look back at my college experience, I would have gone to a less expensive college and been prudent with my student loans usage and read the fine print more carefully. Also, I would not have wasted time taking courses that just bled me all over the place! Thanks for reading my story.

Sincerely,

Juliana.

Juliana provided a great story about education cost in modern society. The main points when seeking a college these days are cost, cost, cost, cost! If one gets a full scholarship at a prestigious university, go all the way. However, if one lacks financial resources, one has the option to apply for a less expensive college. There are many colleges in the United States which provide affordable tuition and excellent education programs.

How is everyone doing in America? Hopefully everyone is doing well. I would first like to introduce myself. My name is Bianca Sommers. I am from the beautiful state of West Virginia where I grew up in a small mining town with a population of about 2,500 people. Although the town is small, everyone knew one another. If one had a problem, neighbors would not mind helping. There was a sense of civic participation and patriotism in the small community. Those were great times which are long gone these days!

Thirty-five years ago, I was born to a third-generation coal mining family. Father was a coal miner, and my mother was a librarian at the local high school. My early childhood was filled with wonderful memories of love, peace, and happiness in my household and community. I would remember every summer my family and I would go to different national parks each year. My parents would rent a cabin for my siblings and I so that we had a chance to experience the outdoors! The family loved the smell of fresh air filling our lungs and the sweet scent of flowers and trees!

I remember like it just happened a few seconds ago my family would gather around a brightly lit campfire. My dad and mother with their cheerful demeanor and southern accent would captivate our imagination with mysteries and scary stories! The night sky would be clear, and the stars would be bright as white precious pearls. Those were the good old days!

When I think of those days I am filled with joy.

Elementary and middle school were great years for my siblings and me. Although the family was always materially comfortable, the most important quality our family shared was love for one another! During my high school years my happy world started to fall apart. When I commenced tenth grade something tragic occurred! On a Tuesday evening I arrived late from cheerleading practice. That Tuesday evening the sky was dark and cloudy. I had arrived home and went to the kitchen to get a snack.

To my surprise I saw my mom sitting on the table weeping. I was completely stunned because I was so accustomed to seeing mom always cheerful. Mom without saying a word stood up and hugged me tightly! A minute had passed, which seemed like a whole eternity before my mom said something. When mom informed me, dad had developed stage four lung cancer, I immediately fell to the floor sobbing!

The next four months the whole family and close friends tried to make my dad's last days as joyous as possible. Dad died on a cold, snowy and freezing night in January. Finally, my dad was at peace. I was relieved dad was not suffering any longer!

Five months after my dad passed away a big economic storm hit the small town without any warning. My father's former company laid off eighty percent of its workforce. Management told the community they had tried to prevent the layoffs, but that globalization and government regulations had made it impossible to compete!

The closing of the plant was devastating for the entire community. A year had passed with many homes abandoned and boarded up because workers had lost their jobs and only source of income. In an instant many of my childhood friends were no longer going to my school.

Let's say that year was particularly hard for my mom, siblings and me. However, due to my family's close relationship with one another we held strong and persevered as a team. To keep our family cohesion strong all of us had assigned chores at home. My brothers' chores included mowing the lawn, cleaning the two bathrooms, and keeping their rooms organized. I on the other hand was responsible for cooking the food mom had seasoned for the day. In addition, I did laundry and made sure the kitchen was spotless. During the weekends I worked as a cashier at a skating rink.

Mom focused on her job and did part time work during the weekends to supplement family income. Every Sunday, our family would go to church. In retrospect faith is what made it easier for my family to continue moving forward.

After graduating from high school like many kids, I did not know what I wanted to do with my life. Mom wanted me to go to college, but I declined. Instead, I worked for two years to get work experience and save money for college. Two years later mom had found a higher paying job in Charleston, West Virginia. Although the commute is about forty minutes my mom was happier because her benefits were much better than her previous job. I also managed to buy my own car, which made me feel quite happy and accomplished.

Two months before the fall classes at the local community college were to begin, I met with Linda who has been an academic counselor for some time. To enroll at the school, I had to take placement tests in subjects like math and English. Linda scheduled my test in two days. Two days later I took the test, and Linda went over the results with me. Linda told me I had excellent mathematical skills and suggested several technical degrees. After evaluating my options, I enrolled in a drafting program specializing in piping design because of low-cost tuition and good job prospects.

The first semester I took two courses because I had not been in school for two years. My first semester I made straight A's on my two courses. Soon spring semester arrived, and I took three more courses. The summer came, and I took a couple of courses, so I would keep up with my graduation target. During the summer I fell in love with a young man named Brad Simeon whom I met in one of my summer drafting classes. I like him because he is smart, has a positive attitude, knows what he wants to do in life and is also very cute! Brad and I continued to go out and enjoy one another's company with the little time we had.

One day I was approached unexpectedly by my academic counselor Linda. Linda informed me that there was an excellent chance to earn a full scholarship because of my good grades. The following week I turned in my application and just waited for a response. A couple of weeks before the second year was about to start, I got a call from Linda on my android phone informing me I had won a full scholarship. I cried out of joy! I told my mother and two siblings I had won the scholarship. All three gave me a big hug. The next day my mother cooked a special meal for the entire family to honor my accomplishments.

Mother encouraged me to quit one of my two jobs, so I could focus on my studies and finish faster. Fortunately, I listened to mom and dropped one of my jobs, which enabled me to take more courses and get better grades. I just had to deal with less disposable income.

So, for the second year I focused on completing my certification. Time passed, Brad and I graduated a year later. After the graduation ceremony, I informed Mother Brad, and I are planning to get married sometime in the future. My mother and brothers were shocked by my announcement. However, all three-ended supporting my decision which I greatly appreciated.

About a month after graduation Brad and I were having trouble finding jobs. However, our luck would change due to Brad's cousin Allen. Allen, informed Brad that there are plenty of jobs in Oklahoma for our profession as piping designers. Allen had been in Oklahoma earning good money for some time. Brad made it clear to me our future prosperity lay in Oklahoma!

After some introspection (women intuition) I knew Brad was right! Therefore, I decided to seek my future economic prospects in Oklahoma. I told mom about going to Oklahoma! Although she did not want me to go, mom knew I would have a better chance of landing a good job in Oklahoma than West Virginia which has suffered economically for years. Like any good mother she told me to be careful.

A week later Brad and I headed west for greener pastures towards Oklahoma. Brad had asked Allen to let us stay at his apartment for a few days till we could find a place to rent. When Brad and I arrived at Allen's

apartment, which was on a sunny Friday evening, both of

us were ecstatic. Allen's apartment is nice, organized, and

clean! In addition, Allen was so kind to have prepared

dinner for Brad and me, which was great! The next two

days Allen showed us around town and the employment

place to apply for on Monday. Personally, Brad and I

could not wait for Monday to arrive so both of us could

start earning money. Monday morning came quickly and

both of us woke up at 5 o'clock in the morning to get

ourselves ready for the day. We showered, ate breakfast,

and had our resumes prepared. By seven the both of us

were out the door!

Brad and I arrived around 7:30 and were the first

ones at the employment office. At eight the interviews

would commence. Both of us were determined to succeed

at all costs! Throughout the day people would be pouring

into the facility looking for work. There were people from

all over the country. Californians, Texans, Floridians, and many countless states who wanted to partake in the fracking boom!   To make a long story short we stayed till five talking to a variety of company human resource managers. A couple of days later we got a call from a company and were hired. Brad told me, and I screamed out of joy. I immediately called my mom and family to inform them of the good news. Mother and my two brothers were extremely excited!

A week later Brad and I started working, which felt great! Three years later Brad and I had learned a lot about our craft and were rewarded. Both of us had made mistakes, but we kept correcting and learning things constantly at the job till we became very proficient in our functions.

After six years Bob and I were transferred to Dallas, Texas and were compensated handsomely! In addition, Brad and I got married and bought a comfortable nice little home in the Dallas suburbs. By this time mom had sold her house in West Virginia and moved to Dallas with my two younger siblings.

Looking back, I am glad I had decided to learn a technical trade. The skills learned at my local community college took me a little over two years, without getting into any debt. By learning a skill in high demand, I was able to find a job quickly and make some decent money without much experience. Now my brothers have followed the same career path and are doing well economically. I am pleased to be an inspiration for my family.

Regards,

Bianca Sommers Drake

Thanks, Bianca, for your true and touching story. Despite all the odds you managed to succeed in your career.

Bianca, you demonstrated that there are a variety of jobs in the market which do not require a four-year degree to have a good paying job!

In the next story a student from Texas will talk about his college education experience. Hello, my name is James. I was born in League City, Texas, a small city south of Houston. During high school, I played football and baseball which made me one of the popular guys in school. Although I was popular I always did well academically, especially in math and science.

In the fifth game of my last football season, I badly injured my knee during a running play. The pain was excruciating! When I received the results from the doctor two weeks later, he informed me I would not be able to play organized football again.

After my diagnosis I started to isolate myself from friends and social activities. As the year progressed, my

grades slowly deteriorated. Where I used to

make A's and Bs turned into C's and D's.

My immediate goal at the time was to

graduate from high school at all costs! I was

excited and relieved when I walked across

the stage and received my high school

diploma.

During the summer I started working

at a home improvement store as a

salesperson. All I was focused on was

getting a new car so I could achieve my

independence. For almost two years I

worked at a home improvement store. My

parents would constantly tell me to go back

to school. At first, I felt annoyed by my

parents' comments about going back to

school, but I relented. In retrospect I am

grateful I had listened to my parents'
judicious advice.

I always knew I wanted to work with
numbers. During the fall I enrolled in a
couple of courses at the local community
college and loved the small classes and
attention. I also found out the courses were
much cheaper than a four-year private or
public university. One of my high school
friends who attended an elite private
university in Texas told me about the tuition
costs and I was mesmerized by the high cost
of education! I am sure glad my high school
friend told me about the high cost of college
so I would avoid a loan pitfall in the future!

The next three years I finished my
associate in engineering and science at my
local community college. I graduated with a

3.8 GPA from my local community college without incurring no debt and a ton of scholarships to the University of Texas at Austin. Two and a half years later I completed my degree in Petroleum engineering debt free! Go Longhorns!!!

Eleven years after graduating from the University of Texas I am making lots of money and have been privileged to travel all over the world at the company's expense! By being debt free, I have been able to buy a nice home and car at a low interest rate.

My advice for students who did not do well in high school for whatever reason is to enroll in a local community college. Attending a community college one can take the same basic courses and save between fifty and sixty percent in tuition costs compared to a public university. In addition, if one decides to change a major during the basics phase at least one will not incur huge amounts of debt! After completing one's basic courses at a community college he or she can transfer to a state college for the final two years without incurring too much debt, which in the long run is a good outcome!

With no or little education debt, it is much easier to buy a new car, start a business, purchase a house, or even take an exotic vacation one has been dreaming about for a long time. Thankfully my knee is fully recovered. These days I swim, hike, and bike to stay in shape. Thanks for reading my story.

As this chapter concludes these are some of the main points to avoid an education nightmare.

1. Look for full ride scholarships, work study programs.

2. Shop around for colleges who have the best financial aid packages.

3. Community college is a great way to save tons of money and offers a gateway to a good public college.

4. If one is going to attain a private loan to finance an education be sure to read the fine print. Look at the amount and interest rate.

5. Choose the amount to be loaned wisely. Remember loans are not free money!! Eventually the education loans must be paid.

6. Take only courses that one needs for a major. Remember the more courses one takes the higher the bill.

7. Unlike other bad debts, student loans cannot be wiped out.

8. Do not fear the trade profession.! Students do not have to complete a four-year degree to get a good job. Most jobs these days require a specific skill that can take at most two years to complete. This means graduating quicker with less debt, which is good for the economy and for the individual.

Remember an education is a critical factor in succeeding in one's life. If an individual plans smartly from the beginning to finance an education, he or she will be better off and happier in the long run with less debt and mental despair!

Chapter 5

Credit Cards

Credit Cards are a part of everyday modern life. When one turns eighteen, credit card companies bombard youths with countless offers and specials. Credit card companies and banks see youth as future consumers and growth potential for decades to come. There must be someone replacing older people as they die each year!

Like anything in life, credit cards have advantages and disadvantages. The main advantage of using credit cards is it helps establish credit. Many people do not realize having a good credit score can simplify one's life. The most important quality of having good credit is low interest rates. Whether buying a house, car, boat, or any product or service, a low interest rate makes it easier for people with great credit to afford the nice things in life.

Now let us get to the disadvantages of owning credit cards. If an individual is a compulsive spender, he or she should stay away from credit cards. Although one can choose to pay the minimum amount, the high interest rates will keep one trapped in a cobweb of debt, which will become difficult to get out of as time passes. Therefore, it is prudent to utilize credit cards wisely or the consequences can be quite severe! The next couple of stories will cover the topic of credit cards.

Good evening, my name is Ariel Dupree. Currently I am forty years old with some white hair, but I am more experienced than in my younger years! Forty years ago, I was born in the magnificent city of Toronto, Canada to a father who

happened to be a family physician and a corporate

attorney mother.

I was blessed by the gods to have an upper middle-

class upbringing. From an early age I was pampered by

both of my parents. The most important blessing is that I

was loved by my mom and dad unconditionally! I can't

complain about my early childhood which was filled with

happiness. However, that changed in a stroke of a

moment. My dad attended a medical conference in Denver

during a cold freezing February filled with snow as white

as the clouds of the heavens.

After the conference had ended my dad ate at an

upscale steakhouse. He must have enjoyed his steak and

vegetables. When dad finished eating his dinner, he left the

restaurant. As he was driving back to the hotel on a quiet

Thursday night filled with a cold wind that penetrates

human bones and a slow pouring light snow, a car slammed

into dad's rental vehicle. All I remember from my mom

was that she told me daddy was not coming back. The

driver who slammed into my dad's vehicle had exceeded

two times the alcohol level in the state of Colorado. I could

see my mom's tears pouring along her beautiful face. She

cried so much it looked like the heavens opened their

humongous gates!

At the time of dad's unexpected passing, I was eight

years old and did not understand the gravity of the

situation. As the seasons came and went, I managed to

cope with dad's loss, but would never forget him! Mother

stayed strong and raised me quite well. My dad's and

mom's parents were very involved in my upbringing,

which helped ease the pain. I also was raised by a great

maid, Maria Velasquez, who would pick me up from

school when mom had to work long late nights to complete

cases. Maria would make sure my homework would be

completed before mom arrived and sometimes Maria had to

raise her voice because I was dancing around instead of doing my homework.

Ever since I was a young girl dancing has always been fun and exciting for me! Dancing would take me to a magical place where all my everyday troubles would be wiped out at least momentarily!   Mom had enrolled me in a dancing academy when I was just six years old. It was like love at first sight! As time passed my dancing ability progressed substantially. I started competing locally in Toronto on different levels of ballroom dancing, winning many accolades. A year before I graduated from high school, I won the national Latin Ballroom dancing award in all of Canada!

The fact I got to that level was due to the support from my family and a small network of close friends. My mother played a crucial part by always encouraging me, even when I self-doubted my dancing abilities. Not to brag, but my mother is a seasoned psychologist who possessed the uncanny ability to read people well, which was

developed as a lawyer through the years of dealing with all

types of characters!

Due to my dancing ability, and impeccable grades

Southern Methodist University in Texas offered me a full

ride scholarship to attend. The first three years went by

quickly, but I had a wonderful time and made plenty of

friends. A couple of days after I finished my third year in

college, I received the somber news from Maria crying

incessantly that my mother had passed away from a

massive heart attack in her law practice. One of the

cleaning ladies who comes at night to clean the offices

found mom slumped in her desk. The ambulance came, but

my mom had been dead for at least a couple of hours.

Hearing the news of mom's untimely passing, my

entire soul collapsed. I was left completely speechless and

shocked beyond description. Fortunately, my roommate

and best friend Erica was with me at the time. Erica could

tell from my facial expression that I was completely distraught! I told Erica, mom had passed away unexpectedly. Tears started to stream from my eyes. Erica stayed quiet and consoled me, which brought some solace to my soul.

With the help of Erica, I managed to get on a flight the next day in the early morning to Toronto. In retrospect my mind went blank due to the intense emotion of losing mom unexpectedly. Maria and my grandparents came towards me when I arrived at the airport. All of them consoled me, which brought relief to my soul!

Fortunately, my mom had taken the necessary precautions and had finalized a trust and the funeral costs had been taken care of beforehand for the entire family. The trauma of losing my father unexpectedly had made my mom determined to be prepared for life's unexpected tragedies. A couple of days passed and I, with the support of family and friends, managed to do a beautiful tribute at the church for my beloved mother. The service for my mom's burial was full! The crowd consisted of family members, friends, associates, and churchgoers.

For the entire summer I stayed in Toronto getting my mom's affairs finalized. My moms' parents blessed their souls stayed with me for six straight weeks offering spiritual and emotional support. My dad's parents would come and visit and talk to me daily.

All I know is that if I did not have the emotional support of my grandparents I would have most likely fallen into a bottomless pit of despair. The three months passed rapidly, and I decided to finish my senior year. My grandparents, Maria, and close friends encouraged me to finish my last year. I had already poured three years of my life and knew I had to keep myself busy or the grief would overtake my soul. As the days turned into weeks and weeks into months the day of my college graduation finally arrived! Before the graduation ceremonies I was thinking how much I had endured in my life losing my parents

unexpectedly, in a moment without saying goodbye to

them. However, I also balanced my soul with the many

accomplishments I had done throughout my life with the

love and support of family and close friends.

As soon as I graduated from college I started

working as a professional dancer for a dance company. My

professional work enabled me to live in a variety of

beautiful and exciting cities such as Miami, Los Angeles,

New York City, and Seattle. Everything seemed to be

going well till I reached the 8th anniversary of my

professional dancing career during a practice run for a

performance show, where I tore my Achilles tendon!

The next day I went to the doctor and explained the

symptoms. She proceeded to do the exams and x-rays on

the ankle. A week later I received the results! To be blunt,

the doctor told me it would be difficult to continue my

professional dancing career. Grudgingly I had to accept my professional dancing career had come to an end.

Although mom had left me with a decent amount of money, in hindsight I was not the best accountant in keeping tabs on my expenses. On the contrary I was naturally a carefree spender who had accumulated ten credit cards before being injured! During my professional dancing years, I rented luxurious apartments and loved the nice things in life which led to me squandering much of my inheritance!

Now reality was staring me in my face! For the first time in my entire life, I had to be more attentive regarding my finances. I was getting healthcare coverage through my dance company, but only for a period before my coverage ended! The time to act was now!! By this point in life my grandparents had passed away due to the ravages of time. God bless their souls!

The only thing I had going for me financially was an overfunded life insurance policy mother had set up for my retirement as a child. My mom told me to never utilize the insurance policy, unless in an extreme emergency! Mother was incessant on me continuing making the premium payments before she passed so that as I got older, I was able to live a comfortable lifestyle. Therefore, dipping into those funds was not an option I was going to do for the foreseeable future!

The first task was to find an affordable place. At the time I hated the idea of moving out of the luxurious apartment, but I had no choice! Sometimes in life one must accept defeat and move forward. In the next couple of months, I found a cute small apartment out in the suburbs with less amenities but managed to save substantially on rent!

During the next couple of months, I was figuring out what I wanted to do with the next chapter of my life. To tell you the truth I was quite afraid of my next career choice! However, I had the determination to succeed whatever life unexpected arrows would throw at me.

I started teaching full time dance to wealthy elderly people and bartend at night to take care of my bills. My focus in the short term was to pay my bills and slow my spending, which was difficult at first. One of my few true friends from the dance company, Elisa, who by nature was a savvy saver helped me along the journey of finally controlling my spending!! Elisa advised me to start paying my smallest credit cards first and that when I finished paying off the credit cards, to discard them! For the next three years I worked in other jobs to get myself out of the credit card debt blackhole!

The next three years were extremely difficult. Many nights I cried by my lonesome self of the hard work I was putting in every day but remained steadfast on getting my financial health in order! After three years of my credit card journey, I managed to whittle down my credit cards substantially.

I still loved nice things, but I was much more cautious with my spending. Also, during this difficult journey I started a small online jewelry business with a friend. Our niche market at the time was young women between ages 25-40 who wanted that independent, confident look. At first, like any other business, it started very slow, only selling to friends and family in the beginning. Although I had left the dance company, I kept in contact with colleagues that allowed me to expand the business by word of mouth. As time progressed the online jewelry business started to pick up exponentially. In retrospect technology makes it much easier than in the past to start a business and reach millions of eyes around the world! A slick website design layout helps a lot!

Nine years after my friend and I commenced the business, the business has grown to twenty-five employees and sales in more than one hundred countries. I also self-taught myself about investing by reading books and attending seminars to take charge of my financial future. The life insurance policy that mom told me not to withdraw for my retirement had grown exponentially! Even credit card big spenders can find redemption if he or she is willing to change. Love you all from Jacksonville, Florida!

Congratulations Ariel! Admire your perseverance, hard work, and tenacity!!

The next story is from Timothy Pemberton who was born and raised in Youngstown, Ohio.

Hello, my name is Timothy Pemberton or Tim for short. I was born in Youngstown Ohio to a hard-working machinist alcoholic, and verbally abusive father and a beautiful, hard-working mother. I was the last of the three children. My mom worked in a Ford assembly plant to feed us and have a roof over our head. My dad drank, gambled, and chased women so he would have very little money left to support the family. When I was five my mom had enough of my dad's shenanigans that she filed for divorce and moved her three children to my grandmother's residence. Although all her children were young at the time, we were glad to leave my dad's presence. Instead of screaming, yelling, and vulgarities my grandma's home was filled with happiness and love.

Even though I was young I knew mom had made the right decision. After leaving my dad for three months our grades and attitude improved dramatically at school. As time passed mom's divorce was finalized! My so-called birth dad did not come to court! He was probably drunk somewhere around town! The judge granted mom full custody of us, which we all celebrated with great joy! My siblings and I did not need to see our irresponsible dad again. As the years passed my oldest brother went to college on an army ROTC scholarship and graduated as an engineer and made a career in the Army Corps of Engineers. My mom, grandmother, sister, and I were so proud of my brother. A couple of years later my sister graduated as a teacher, but my grandmother was not in attendance because she had passed away a year earlier. God bless my beautiful grandmother's soul a wonderful loving lady I will never forget!

The only person left to walk along the graduation podium was myself. Unlike my two elder siblings I focused on a two-year technical degree specializing in mechanical drafting. Since I was a young kid, I always loved drawing a variety of things such as buildings and landscapes. Although my mom had encouraged me to go into architecture, I did not want to go to school for five years accumulating large education debts like my other peers! Besides I wanted to make money quickly! My mom accepted my decision and after three years of studying and working full time I graduated with my associate degree in drafting. My family and I were quite ecstatic! However, during my time in college and beyond I developed a problem with credit cards.

When I started college, I was naïve about credit cards like so many kids across the country. I just knew I could utilize a credit card to purchase something I wanted and pay it later. If I just paid the minimum balance, I would be okay. Boy I was wrong by a mile. Five years after graduating from college I was working in Cleveland as a draftsman making six figure money and spending like crazy.

One moment I was employed, and the next moment I was laid off because projects were canceled due to the downturn of the economy during the so-called "Great Recession". I was shocked and the only thing I had was a little savings, huge amounts of credit card debt and a 401-k plan that would be decimated in the coming months!

The only thing I had left was my pride. In the meantime, I was forwarding my resume to other prospective employers every night. I was aware this would be a difficult job market.

The next year was quite difficult, probably one of the hardest years of my life. I had to move back with my mother to Youngstown because I was unable to pay my rent! I felt like a complete failure! Looking back, I was fortunate because a lot of acquaintances did not have the luxury to stay at their parents' residence. My mom did not seem bothered by my presence. Mother loved that I was at grandmothers' house because my mother felt she was accompanied by someone physically. By this time my mom had retired from the plant and was receiving her pension. Although my mom had retired, she was still working for the city of Youngstown to keep busy. Mother always told my siblings and I that when she retired, a part time job would be an ideal situation because she wanted to make a little extra to spend on the grandkids and be away from the house.

By the end of the third week of having moved back home to Youngstown, I had managed to find a full-time job as an assistant manager at a local grocery store! I was extremely lucky due to the fact the former assistant manager had been promoted to manager in another state just a month ago. I had been out of work for a year and two months.

The first action I took was to declare bankruptcy. I knew my credit would be destroyed in the short term, but in the long term I would start all over again with a clean slate. Anyway small, medium, and large businesses go bankrupt everyday throughout the year why can't I. Therefore, I did not feel any regret!

Another action I took in my financial renaissance was to keep track of my spending. Unlike in the past where

I was completely disorganized with my spending, I developed the discipline and skill to track my spending over time! Living within one's means was my grandmother's mantra for my siblings and me. Looking back, I should have listened to grandmother's advice who was a child of the Great Depression, but like most young people I thought I knew everything under the heavens! I must admit I was a financial knucklehead!

The next seven years I grew financially smarter and wealthier. I had worked my way up to grocery regional director in the beautiful city of Tampa, Florida. For the last two years I had been living in gorgeous Tampa and managed to buy a small townhome about twenty minutes from work. By living closer to work I saved on gas and did not have to worry about traffic. Thankfully I had built up my 401-k, bought some gold and silver and had only one credit card! I would pay my balance in full instead of paying the minimum balance. I was not going to let credit high interest rates, kill me. I learned my lesson the hard

way!   Love from Tampa!

CREDIT CARDS LESSONS LEARNED

1. Good way to acquire credit history for future
   purchases such as car loans and home
   mortgages.
2. Use credit cards only if one knows he or she can
   pay the full balance. Remember by paying the
   minimum balance debt increases due to high
   interest rates! This means more stress and
   difficulty to pay debt in the future!
3. The more credit cards one has the higher
   possibility of financial anguish and distress in
   the future!

Chapter 6

Changing One's mindset and Environment to Improve Physical Health

Another important factor in one's

life is to be physically fit. The more

physically fit a person is the more

productive and less costly for employers. Healthier workers, students, and entrepreneurs on average tend to perform better than unhealthy people. Being healthy also improves one's quality of life. When a person is healthy, he or she has more energy, is positive, confident, and can enjoy many of life's benefits!

Many of today's diseases can be attributed to the obesity epidemic which is growing exponentially worldwide. Diseases that can be attributed to obesity are diabetes, heart disease, and certain cancers. Therefore, it is imperative for everyone to start reaching their healthy weight.

To lose weight, one must change his or her mindset and environment. The next couple of stories will demonstrate how changing one's mindset can improve quality of life!

Hello, my name is Joseph. I am from Philadelphia, Pennsylvania, the city of brotherly love. Since I was a teenager, I have been a bit overweight. Although I was overweight, I participated in a myriad of sports such as baseball, football, and volleyball.

However, when I went to college my weight ballooned greatly. I was eating badly and not doing any physical activity. When I graduated from college, I weighed 350 lbs. at six feet! At that critical point of my life, I decided to change my health trajectory.

When I arrived home my family was surprised, I had gained so much weight. I hated it, but one must accept the truth, to get ahead. In the first month I started a walking regimen at a neighborhood park early in the morning around five for twenty minutes. To tell you the truth I was winded. That was sad, but I persisted. During the first month I lost fifteen pounds but knew I still had a long way to go. Two months later I gained weight once again!

The main culprit of my weight gain was my diet. In the refrigerator there was too much temptation like white bread, chocolate chip cookies, soda water, and other stuff. I would binge at night like crazy. Even though I tried not to eat unhealthy foods, my will would succumb to the junk food temptations!

Therefore, I decided I had to move out of my parents' home. Fortunately, by this time I had found a job as a database administrator and was able to rent an apartment close to my job. In addition to living by myself, I started cooking my own food, which consisted of protein, fruit, and vegetables. At first, I was awkward with my cooking. However, I was persistent and determined to succeed at all costs! Three months after I left home, I lost about fifty pounds and felt much better and had more energy. A year and a half later I weighed a fit and trim 195 lbs.!

I was so excited and felt I had regained my life back. Geez I was slimmer than anytime during my youth! I finally realized that the root cause of my overweight dilemma was my household environment.

Due to my dramatic weight loss, I was getting all sorts of positive attention from coworkers, family, and close friends. I would tell them I changed my environment and was persistent in losing weight. I gave my mom a lot of tips on food preparation and in six months both my parents lost a significant amount of weight. Their blood pressure and sugar improved significantly, which made me very happy.

I am also in the process of getting married to the love of my life in a couple of months. I wholeheartedly believe one must decide to change one's environment to see progress. Thanks for reading my story.

What a lovely story.

Congratulations! For most of his life Joseph has been overweight. Like a lot of us who struggle with weight problems it can sometimes feel like a daunting task to lose the unwanted pounds. Joseph demonstrated that if one wants to lose weight, he or she must decide to change their mind and environment.

Hello everyone, my name is Allison, and I am proud to be from the beautiful state of Mississippi. Since I was a little girl, I competed in hundreds of beauty pageants. My parents wanted me to be a top model for an elite model agency in New York at all costs. At first, I loved the pageants because I was the center of attention. I would be pampered and treated like a little princess while traveling across the United States and having the opportunity to meet countless people.

During my senior year in high school, I was chosen as prom queen of my school. I had grown into a six-foot slim naturally blonde with sparkling blue eyes who played varsity soccer and ran track for my school. When I graduated from high school, I received a call from a top modeling agency in New York informing me I had a job with them. My parents were jubilant and excited!

I was excited, but at the same time apprehensive. I desperately wanted to go to the University of Alabama who had accepted me into the premed program. However, I relented to my parents' wishes.

The first year was tough as can be expected, however, the money was great. The second to fourth year I got more work and traveled to a myriad of beautiful places across the globe! During this time, I was having difficulty maintaining my bodyweight. At times I would be so hungry that I would just binge on food!

Anytime I gained even five pounds my agent would put pressure on me to lose weight quickly. Soon I was utilizing illegal drug substances which would lead to my eventual decline. I was living a fast life, filled with fun and danger. At the same time, I knew that if I did not find help soon, I would eventually die!

Fortunately, I met an angel called Eric who changed and saved my life. I met Eric at an art gallery. When I first laid eyes on Eric, I saw that he was quite handsome. However, the quality that made him attractive was his calm demeanor. To make

a long story short Eric and I hit it off very

good. After some time had elapsed, I told

Eric I was hooked on drugs!

With Eric's encouragement I

checked into a rehabilitation center leaving

my modeling career. I knew my parents

would be deeply disappointed by my

decision, but I had to make a change. It was

tough to accept I had fallen from my lofty

pedestal all the way to the abyss! Six months

passed and I was climbing upwards from my

addiction. I also confronted my bulimic

disease which I had avoided for a long time.

The savings that I had from my

modeling job I decided to go to Seattle,

Washington and attend college. Eric had

invited me for many months to come with

him to Seattle because that is where he has his house and art studio. I just wanted to get away from the craziness of New York City! Along my journey to recovery Eric supported me emotionally, which was the greatest gift of all. There are not words to describe how lucky and grateful I am to have met Eric. Five years passed and I finished my degree in Biology. A day after I graduated, I married Eric, the love of my life. A year later our son Julius, which is our most important emerald in the world, was born.

Currently I am director of a substance abuse center and am passionate about helping people recover from their addiction. Now I am healthier and have finally found myself after walking blind for so long!

The human mind is a powerful force to be reckoned with. Allison demonstrated a will to change her mental state and environment. Allison also had a strong support group and Eric to help her conquer the inner demons within her soul. Key concepts.

1. One must accept there is a problem! That is the first important step to make a change.

2. Take small steps to get to one's overall goals.

3. One's environment must be modified to succeed. If one keeps living in the same environment it will be difficult to progress!

Chapter 7

Nutrition

Food is a big part of world culture. Television, internet, and radio ads constantly bombard people with messages to convince them to eat food and beverages. People need food to stay alive and keep their bodies functioning properly. The problem in modern society is that people consume too much processed foods.

Because our lives move so rapidly many of us have forgotten the essentials of healthy cooking. Instead, modern society has chosen fast food to fill the void of our appetites. By choosing unhealthy food many developed and developing countries are facing rising health care costs due to the obesity epidemic. Being overweight or obese can lead to many horrible diseases such as diabetes, cardiovascular disease, depression, gut issues, and many forms of cancer. All these diseases are major cause of death every year.

In addition to the diseases mentioned above, one's quality of life is affected by poor eating habits! This means it can be difficult to carry one's grandkids, walk in the park and enjoy the majestic and spectacular sounds of nature, bowling, going out to dance, or many beautiful social activities one takes for granted. It is estimated that seventy to seventy five percent of our body composition is due to nutrition. The rest is due to exercise and genetics. So, if one can get nutrition in track most of the work is done for a healthy body! It sounds simple, but difficult to implement. However, if one achieves a long-term goal of losing weight people will be healthier, sexier, and more confident. The next two stories will illustrate how nutrition plays an integral part in overall health.

Hello everyone. I hope all of you have had a spectacular day filled with happiness and love. My name is Susan. I am from the beautiful city of Jacksonville, Florida. Since I was a young girl, I have always been active and full of energy. During high school I played volleyball and the flute.

After high school I attended the University of Arizona where I was active and able to maintain an athletic physique. My friends and I would go to the mountains on the weekends and hike all around the Phoenix area enjoying the beautiful scenery.

Immediately after completing nursing school, my first job was as an emergency room nurse working the graveyard shift at a private hospital in sunny San Diego, California. The physician I was going to work with on a consistent basis is a young doctor who had just finished his residency in California.

At first the job was stressful, but I slowly adapted to the work environment. Three years after I met the young doctor whose first name is Luke, he and I got married. I guess it's true that love can happen at any time! Well two years later we had two female twins. Those two girls are the most important treasure in the world for us. Luke, after working for some time, started a private practice with four of his medical school friends at the hospital. I stayed at home for about one year to take care of the kids.

Around this time, I had gained a lot of weight due to pregnancy, eating way too much, and lack of exercise. Even Luke had gained weight around his once trim waist. I guess the stress of raising a family and work contributed to our weight gain. Neither Luke nor I wanted to accept we had gotten our bodies way out of proportion.

However, the weight scales and mirror don't lie. I was forty pounds overweight, and Luke had gained about fifty pounds! Just like me Luke felt sluggish and tired all the time. On a Sunday morning I told Luke we needed to be an example to our patients and two young daughters by losing weight. That same day both of us were on a mission to eat better and increase our physical activity!

This meant that buffets had to go and portion control was slowly implemented. Luke and I had to cook more of our food at home! The first week Luke and I developed a strategy to prepare our food on Sundays. Essentially my beloved and I would prepare food for the next four to five days in about three hours. Both of us would season our chicken, fish, and lean meats, with herbs and spices. In addition to seasoning the protein, both of us would cut up the vegetables into smaller pieces so it would be easier to cook. When the seasoning was completed my husband, and I stored the food in Tupperware boxes to preserve the flavor for the coming days. All we had to do was cook the food. Both of us would either bake or grill our delicious meats, seafood, and steam the vegetables.

During the next six months my husband and I were seeing results. Luke had dropped forty pounds and me about thirty-five pounds. In addition, a workout regimen which emphasized total body movements was done early in the morning three times a week. Also, both of us only drank water or black coffee without sugar.

Ever since Luke and I modified our nutritional choices we have increased our energy exponentially! My husband, kids and I rarely eat out anymore except on special occasions such as going to the ballet, theatre, or other social function. Instead, my husband and I are expanding our cooking repertoire with healthy cuisines. People say cooking is work, but for my husband and I cooking is romantic! When both of us are preparing the food we talk, joke around, and enjoy each other's company.

Overall, nutrition should be the most important issue for families because it is where all of us attain energy for our daily activities. Without

proper nutrition, people will not be able to perform

well. Remember the adage health is wealth. I wish

everyone in the world a great and healthy year!!

Sincerely,

Susan

Thanks, Susan, for the wonderful story!
Susan's story demonstrates one must change
nutritional habits to see progressive gains. In the
next story an individual named Marco will describe
how nutrition changed his life and family.

Hello everyone, my name is Marco. I am
from the beautiful windy city of Chicago.
My grandparents legally emigrated from
Mexico to the United States when they were
quite young. The old folks first ended up in
the beautiful and mesmerizing state of

California filled with mountains that touch

the heavens and skies as blue as the

Caribbean Sea. Both of my grandparents

stayed in California for about five years

working daily to support a growing family.

As time passed my grandfather was

hired to work at a manufacturing plant in Chicago

which offered great benefits. My grandfather and

his family packed up their bags and went to Illinois

to start a new life. Although Chicago's frigid winter

is quite cold and imposing, the young family

continued to thrive. My grandmother also started to

work at a small manufacturing plant. Four years

after working at the plant my grandmother saved

enough money to open a restaurant. Mom and her

two brothers would help grandmother on the

weekends.

Grandmother wanted her kids to develop a strong work ethic and mental toughness for life's obstacles! The strong work ethic mentality enabled my mom and two uncles to graduate from college. Mom's first job after college was as a high school science teacher. In the first year of her teaching career, she met dad who was a math teacher at the same high school. A couple of years later I was born. Two years later my sister joined the family.

When I graduated from high school I did not want to go to college. As one can imagine my parents were deeply disappointed with my decision. Mom and dad around this time had risen to high school principals at two Chicago public schools. My parents always inculcated in me and my sister the importance of education. At first, I wanted to become an engineer. However, all that changed in my senior year of high school. Out of curiosity my best friend and I enrolled in a cooking class. At the time I just wanted to get an easy A to improve my GPA score. As the course progressed, I became almost obsessed with preparing and cooking food.

I would experiment with a variety of spices to find different flavors. My classmates and instructor loved the dishes I prepared for them. Moving forward my goal in life was to be a chef! Thankfully my high school cooking instructor guided me on the right path. The instructor provided scholarship information for cooking school and helped me land a job during the summer at an exclusive restaurant in Chicago.

I learned a lot during those three months on how an exclusive restaurant is run efficiently. Having worked at my grandmother's restaurant in the past made it easier to understand the intricacies of how everything is put together. During my off time I would read books about the importance of healthy nutrition for the body and soul.

The next two years I immersed myself in cooking school and learned the details of manipulating a variety of foods, tastes, and flavors. Also, during this great time of my life, I managed to reach my ideal weight. All I did was to eat less, cut refined sugars, drink more water and reduce carb intake. I also did cardio boxing three times a week, which has given me extra energy throughout the entire day. My mood and personality have become more outgoing due to weight loss and exercise. Although I feel great, I am elated my family members have learned from me to eat healthier, thus improving their quality of life!

I am happy to report mom and dad have lost weight. Their blood sugar and pressure are in the normal range once again! Both of my parents have cut eating out, which has benefitted them financially and health wise. Instead, my parents are cooking their meals in a healthier manner. My grandparents take spinning classes together three times a week and are active in their humongous garden where they grow fruits and vegetables that glow, which bedazzles the human senses! Finally, my sister thanked me for helping her lose weight. My sister is now a more confident young woman filled with optimism, energy and happiness due to better nutrition.

I graduated from cooking school as the top student of the class and found a nice job at an exclusive hotel. Eight years after graduating from cooking school, I have risen to master chef and have received glowing reviews from many prestigious outlets. When I am not working, I volunteer for the American Diabetes Association by teaching people to cook simple healthy recipes. Teaching people to eat nutritiously is not only a passion of mine, but also an obsession. Life is beautiful! Thanks for taking the time to read my story. Love from the magnificent city of Chicago.

Sincerely,

Marco

Wonderful story! The beautiful part is that Marco shared his love for healthy nutrition with family and strangers. Marco' story demonstrates that one person can convince many people to make healthier choices. The important concepts to take from this chapter on nutrition will be described in the following list.

1. Nutrition is a key component of who we are. Remember nutrition is 70 to 80 percent of how we look!

2. To lose weight, one must slowly reduce portion size. It is more important to make small incremental changes which will last a lifetime.

3. When one cooks at home a household saves money which can be utilized to cook healthier food. By

eating healthier one will have less
diseases and pain in the future!

4. Try to make water the drink one
   consumes eighty percent of the time.
   Remember water has zero calories.
   Water helps remove toxins from the
   human body.

5. Eat baked, steamed, or grilled foods.
   In addition, consume more protein,
   vegetables, healthy fats, and grains.
   Eat fruit moderately.

6. Keep improving healthy nutrition
   every day. The results will show
   over time.

CHAPTER 8

Sleep and Exercise

In modern society it can be difficult to get any exercise due to many modern conveniences such as public transport, cars, airplanes, boats and other modes of transportation. In addition, all of us have modern entertainment options such as video games, television, laptops, and social media which take away time from physical activities. Although our lives have been made easier by modern technology humanity has become less healthy. Many people have sick days due to being obese or overweight. If companies could minimize sick days, health care costs would diminish significantly, productivity rise, and profits improve!

Countless studies have demonstrated that regular exercise strengthens our body, mind, and can help prevent a variety of diseases such as diabetes, heart disease, and many cancers. Most people believe one must go to the gym and workout for hours seven days a week to be healthy. One does not have to labor in a gym for hours. Exercise can be done at home, hotel, outdoors, and millions of other places too much to name.

Another component of having a healthy body is getting adequate sleep. Remember robust and lean muscles do not grow during exercise. Muscle growth occurs when one is at rest! When one does not sleep properly, the body has difficulty in repairing its cells which can lead to sickness down the road. Also, when sleep is neglected people tend to eat more, thus gaining weight. Therefore, sleep is imperative! The next couple of stories will demonstrate the importance of exercise and sleep.

My name is Matthew. Currently I am an investment advisor for a large brokerage company in New York City. Originally, I am from Honolulu, Hawaii. Ever since I was a young kid my friends and I would wake up early in the morning before school to surf and enjoy the beautiful beach.

As I got older, I became very good at baseball. I earned a scholarship to play baseball for the University of Nebraska. The four years in Nebraska came and went quickly and I attained a degree in accounting. A month after graduating, I landed a job as a loan officer for an Indianapolis bank. When a year had passed, I was transferred to another position as financial analyst for the bank. Six months later I passed the series 7 and 66 licenses. As a financial analyst I worked long hours ensuring the bank was getting its money's worth on investments.

During this period of long hours, I would eat anything. My routine would be to get a couple of drinks and something to eat after work. When I would get home from my long and stressful job, I would set up my alarm and crash for the night. I was making good money so I could afford to eat out every day. A couple of years passed, and I had gained forty-five pounds! The once slim thirty-two-inch waist and athletic physique had gone down the tubes. Just focusing on my position to climb the ranks and earn lots of money was my primary goal!

The hard work finally paid off in the long run. Five years after I became an analyst, a large brokerage firm wanted me to work for them. I would have great benefits and paid much higher if I went to New York City. The brokerage firm would pay all my moving costs. When I heard the great news, I was ready to go to New York City.

On the last day in Indianapolis, I looked at the bathroom mirror carefully and was quite unhappy with my portly body. Going forward I was going to change my lifestyle!

When I arrived in New York City I settled into a nice apartment. I resolved to start cooking my food once again and hopefully get more sleep than in the past. Also, I decided that I was going to start working out three times a week in the morning.

The Sunday before I was about to commence work for my new employer, I spent about three hours preparing my food for the week. The first week I attended orientations to learn about the company's culture and procedures. Two weeks after the company orientation I had lost about three pounds.

To lose unwanted weight, I had to be persistent and patient. As the days turned to weeks and weeks to months the weight started to drop dramatically. A year after I started my lifestyle changes, I had lost all the weight and was trim again. I lifted three times a week and focused on compound movements such as squats, pull-ups, dips, rows, and bench presses. These types of movements work large muscle groups which help burn fat and build lean muscle.

I also joined a dancing class during the weekends to incinerate even more fat and improve flexibility. In addition, I stopped drinking and was getting much more sleep. My energy, enthusiasm, and work have improved substantially. Although the job has a lot of stress, I have managed to deal better with the pressure of my position. Well, that is all I have to say. Thanks for reading my story and may all of you find true happiness.

What a wonderful and inspirational story. The next story is also very inspirational and heartwarming.

Howdy everyone, my name is Catherine. I am originally from Des Moines, Iowa but presently reside in Austin. I love Austin's nightlife and festive atmosphere. Currently I am blessed to have a beautiful eight-year-old boy. Just five years ago I was overweight, and unfortunately had a small stroke. For a moment I thought my life would be coming to an end. That day would change the rest of my life!

Nine years ago, I graduated from the University of Iowa and was ready to embark on my new career. My best friend was going to Austin because she had found a job as a high school science teacher. Sonya invited me to Austin. Although I did not have a job at the time, Sonya was sure I would find a position quickly. I had never been to Texas and was ready for a new adventure! I told my parents about my decision to leave Iowa and the Midwest for a better future.

My parents supported me, and a week later Sonya and I were on our way to Texas. When Sonya and I arrived in Austin both of us were surprised how beautiful the city is with its spectacular hills, well-manicured lawns, homes, and historical edifices. Sonya and I quickly found a small, but comfortable apartment. In less than a week Sonya and I discovered an interesting nightlife Austin had to offer. The first couple of months after we arrived, I found a job as a programmer analyst for a state agency and over time grew to love my job.

Sonya also started working as a high school science teacher. I guess we were two young beautiful women on the rise. A year later I met a guy named Michael via an acquaintance at a nice excusive jazz club.

The jazz music was smooth, captivating,

hypnotic, and the singer performed

excellently! I was surprised by how well

Michael danced.

The next six months the both

of us developed an intense and passionate

relationship. When the six months had

passed, I noticed that I was pregnant. When

I told Michael the news, he appeared to be

happy at first. However, as time passed, I

could tell that Michael tried to ignore me at

all costs! I should have listened to my

female instincts that the relationship was

ending, but I refused! Six months after I had

the baby Michael informed me via text, he

wanted to end the relationship. Instantly I

texted Michael back and informed him I would initiate child support!

Unfortunately, to cope with my breakup, I neglected exercise, proper sleep, and was eating poorly. Thankfully mom offered to help babysit my child for a time, while I was at work. Sonya, my best friend, did her best to get me out of my depression. When I had come to Austin, I was five foot three weighing a hundred ten pounds. In three and a half years after my son's birth I had gained one hundred pounds! Looking back, I feel so ashamed of myself for letting down my loved ones, especially my son.

I remember just before my heart attack Sonya had invited me many times to take a walk in the park with her to start an exercise regimen. I would always tell Sonya

I was busy! I was at my desk when I started

to have a horrible headache and difficulty

breathing. I then fainted. Thankfully one of

my coworkers knew CPR or I would be six

feet under the ground. In the next couple of

weeks, I slowly recovered.

The doctors told me if I failed

to lose weight, get enough sleep, and

minimize my stress I would not live very

long. The message from the doctors who

were attending me during my recovery

phase was a wakeup call to action. When I

arrived home, I had lost about ten pounds

during my hospital stay. I was so happy to

see my son and could see his tears running

down his handsome face. I hugged him so

hard and promised my beloved son I was going to change my lifestyle.

I could see that Sonya and my mom were also pouring tears of joy and knew the old optimistic Catherine was back with a vengeance! In the next year I focused on being healthy and fit totally for my son, loved ones, and myself! I completely changed my nutrition and was eating healthier food. All the processed and junk foods were old history.

I started a circuit training class which used weights and one's own bodyweight. To tell you the truth, that first day was hell!! When I came out of the training, I was hooked on the class and continued for months. In addition to circuit training, I do yoga twice a week with Sonya to improve flexibility and balance. By getting healthier all my loved ones have become healthy as well.

I also have been sleeping much better which has helped improve my memory and reduce cravings. Three years later I am in the best shape of my entire life! There are not words that can express how fortunate I was to have a support group which enabled me to rise from the ashes!

Now that was a great story. Catherine had a lot of obstacles but managed to persevere with the encouragement of loved ones. Catherine was focused on getting her health back for her son, family, and friends. The story is very touching indeed! The main points to learn about exercise and sleep are the following.

1. One must make sure to get adequate sleep. Sleep is when the body repairs itself from the mental and physical stresses it faces each day! Remember lean muscles are built during sleep. Not during exercise.

2. Adequate sleep helps with hormonal balance and prevents people from overeating which can lead to weight gain!

3. The main goal is to keep moving. Minimize television and other social media. There is time during the day. Remember one must take the initiative! Even if one starts exercising fifteen minutes a day, that is progress.

4.   Be patient and persistent. One does not want to start fast and then injure oneself. By injuring oneself it delays progress and can take longer to see results.

5.   There is a variety of exercise regiments one can do. For example, weight training, yoga, aerobics, biking, swimming, dancing, walking, and many others that are too much too name! Consult a physician before commencing an exercise regimen.

6.   Read and educate oneself about the different exercise programs. Make sure to choose exercise programs one will enjoy for the long term.

Chapter 9

Retirement and

Savings

Currently many people do not plan for retirement.

What many people fail to realize is that after a certain

amount of time has passed, he or she is far behind in their

retirement goals. By being behind in his or her retirement goals, many retirees across the developed world are forced to work way past their retirement years in fear he or she might outlive their income! Studies have shown that sixty-six percent of baby boomers retirement funds are grossly underfunded with an average of just ten thousand dollars!

Due to the financial damage caused by the Great Recession millions of Americans have left the stock market. Many retirees are facing mountains of debt such as credit cards, mortgages, car notes, and student loans which were used to help their kids and grandkids! In addition to debt, retirees are also facing inflation that crushes fixed income and makes everyday essentials expensive! Also adding to financial displacement is the disappearance of pensions. Pensions were once commonplace in the past, and helped provide a buffer for many retirees, but these days are a relic! In the next few stories, I will provide why planning for retirement early in one's working career can save a lot of pain down the road!

Hi, everyone, my name is Simon Chevalier. I was born in Baton Rouge, Louisiana to parents who worked their entire lives in the oil industry. My dad worked as a roughneck and my mother as a sales manager for a global oil conglomerate. I cannot complain about the oil business which provided a comfortable upbringing for our family. My parents, siblings, and I had the pleasant comforts of life such as a roof over our head, electricity, clean water, delicious food consisting of exotic meats, fruits, and vegetables, pleasant deserts, vacations and many more! Even though we were raised in a comfortable environment our parents pushed my siblings and I hard to succeed academically.

Looking back, I am greatly indebted that mother and father taught my siblings and I the value of hard work at an early age!   As the hourglass of time passed my siblings, parents and I got older. The siblings consisted of

three brothers including myself. I was the oldest of the

brothers. My other brothers were a couple of years younger

than I. It was like a dream how fast we grew up from

toddlers to young adults. My brothers and I graduated from

Tulsa University in Oklahoma with degrees in engineering

with honors. Both of my younger siblings specialized in

computer and electrical engineering, while I specialized in

mechanical and petroleum engineering.

As soon as I graduated from Tulsa University my

first job assignment was Saudi Arabia. I loved going to

Saudi Arabia and became enthralled with the people, food,

culture and its beautiful architecture. During those five

years I enjoyed every moment of my career! When the five

years had elapsed, I was sent back to the states and spent

my money foolishly like many young people have done in

the past. I had made so much money during my so-called

self-exile I did not know what to do with cash. Two

months after arriving in the United States I bought a fancy sports car, expensive clothes, and would go clubbing with friends almost every weekend. Everything in my life was going well!

Then one day out of nowhere I was laid off from my high paying job during February 1982, which was brutal! Millions of people around the world lost their jobs, which affected families immensely! The early eighties recession was the worst recession since the horrible Great Depression! For the next eight months I struggled to find a job in my engineering profession. I tried everything like going to job fairs, trainings, sending resumes to hundreds of companies across the United States, and networking to no avail.

Fortunately, I was able to find three part time jobs to pay my bills, which unfortunately do not stop when one loses his or her job! During 1982 I promised myself every day that I would be more cautious with my money in the future. In retrospect nineteen eighty-two was the toughest year financially in my entire life!

Soon 1982 passed (good riddance) and a new year started with fresh hope and optimism. Three months into the year I got an unexpected call from an engineering company in Michigan who wanted to schedule a phone interview the following day. The interviewer told me the company had a job opening and was very impressed by my education and work experience. Eventually the interview went better than expected and I was hired. One major lesson I learned during my tough economic Odyssey was that one day a person can be financially comfortable, and the next day be struggling! I made an oath to myself never to be caught with my pants down financially ever again! So, for the next five years I worked in Detroit building my career and depleted savings. Due to working eighty hours per week and meeting deadlines consistently, I was promoted to the Los Angeles, California office to lead the engineering department of the company.

Seven months elapsed and I was invited to speak at an inner-city high school in Los Angeles about high paying math and science careers. When the presentation came to its conclusion, the young teenagers gave a huge round of applause. About fifteen questions were asked by the curious students. I answered all fifteen questions to the best of my ability. After I had finished answering the students' questions one of the assistant principals came over to congratulate me on the presentation. The assistant principal Nadia Shipley and I immediately clicked!

Two years later I got married and had a beautiful gorgeous only child daughter Madeline. I had managed to purchase a modest house in the suburbs. During the first year of Madeleine's young life, Nadia stayed home full-time to take care of our lovely daughter. I took care of all our expenses. Although Nadia stayed home, she managed to learn about financial topics that would pay great dividends in the coming years for the entire family! Nadia taught me a lot about investing which sparked my imagination.

As the seasons came and went rapidly a lot of life events occurred. Both of my parents had passed away and my wife's dad had died as well. Unfortunately, as one accumulates wisdom loved ones are lost along the journey of life! The youngest of my brothers developed stage two colon cancer but was able to recover successfully and has been cancer free ever since. My mother-in-law sold her residence and moved in with my wife and me. Also, by this time my daughter Madeline has grown into a smart, independent and beautiful young woman who only needs one more year at the University of Michigan to graduate from dental school without incurring any financial debt! Fortunately, Madeline had done well academically during her undergraduate studies which enabled her to receive a full ride scholarship with all expenses paid. My wife had retired from the public education profession in 2007 when the so called "Great Recession" threw the world into economic darkness!

During this point in time, I had changed companies, and was working with an international oil company as vice president of operations. From 2007 – 2009 people were being laid off by the hundreds of thousands on a weekly basis. The unemployment rate in the United States during the Great Recession had reached about seventeen percent if one includes people not actively looking for a job opening. It seemed that the whole world was going to tilt toward a repeat of the Great Depression of 1929. Thank God it did not!

This time I was prepared to deal with life's unexpected obstacles. I was determined never to suffer financially again like I had in 1982 when I was a young inexperienced twenty-seven-year-old kid! So, for the next thirty years my wife and I focused on saving and investing our money wisely to retire earlier and enjoy the beautiful things in life such as traveling. One of the first actions that my wife and I did during 1990 was to purchase a twenty-unit apartment rundown complex in Pasadena, Texas. A remodeling crew was hired to do the work at an economical price. Three months later the apartment unit was opened for business.

The rent money was utilized to pay the bank loans. Five years later my wife and I were debt free and growing our cash flow. By 2007 my wife and I had about two hundred apartment units in Texas even though we were living in California. I also have a 401-k plan with the company. In addition, my wife and I have overfunded life insurance policies, bitcoin, expensive wine bottles, art collections, gold and silver coins, and farmland to increase our retirement income as we progress in age. From 2008 to 2014 I invested as much as possible to maximize my family retirement income. Fortunately, due to the Federal reserve's low interest rates my financial assets increased in value once again!

By February 2016 I decided to retire with assistance from my lovely wife and a team of retirement specialists. My wife and I decided that it was time to move to Texas. The prominent reasons were to be closer to my daughter's young family, and affordability. So, in March of 2016 our house was put up for sale. For the next six months my wife and I looked across Texas to see where we wanted to spend our retirement years!

After much thought my wife and I decided to move to a nice town about forty minutes away from downtown Corpus Christi. Together we bought a seven-acre spread that came with a three thousand square foot one story house consisting of five bedrooms, two and a 1/2 bathrooms, entertainment room, a beautiful kitchen and an attached garage. My wife and I plan to grow a fruit and vegetable garden that will entertain us and my mother-in-law.

An extra bonus in moving to Texas is that my daughter has her dental practice and lives close to San Antonio with her husband and my two beautiful grandkids. By December 2016 my wife, mother-in-law, and I had moved to Texas just in time to celebrate the Holidays. Looking back, I am grateful to have lost my job in 1982 because it opened my eyes to the importance of money and investments in one's life. In my sixty-three years of life, tough experiences will mold a wiser person in the long run. Thanks for reading my story.

Simon faced adversity in his young career and was able to live a comfortable retirement by having a long-term plan, patience, and diversifying assets! In the next story a young woman is trying to prepare herself for retirement.

Hello, my name is Rebecca from Charlotte, North Carolina. I grew up in a middle-class family where my mother and father worked their entire lives for the United States Postal Service. Both of my parents before joining the postal service served for five years in the United States Air Force right after finishing high school. My parents always told my younger brother and I that they were privileged and grateful to have served in the Air Force.

Fortunately, I was brought up in a loving and caring family. My family and I lived within two miles of my mom and dad's parents. Growing up, I preferred to play video games and work in our back yard garden. My grandparents were children of the Great Depression who had lived on a small farm and were able to grow their own food and sell the extra harvest for profit during those difficult times. I also learned from my grandparents about the basics of money, value of hard work, discipline, and patience!

At fifteen years old, my first job was working at McDonald's after school because I wanted to make money on my own! For two years I worked at McDonald's and learned that for an organization to succeed one must surround themselves with people who are dedicated one hundred percent! During my time at McDonald's, I put part of my money in the company's 401 k plan and the other amount in a savings account.

Also, during ninth grade I was introduced to computer programming and fell instantly in love! Dad, seeing my enthusiasm, bought me a personal computer to use for school. For the next four years I delved into programming and learned to think in an analytical way to solve problems, which made learning other computer languages easier.

After finishing high school, I went straight to work. My parents were very disappointed with my decision to forgo college and tried on many occasions to convince me. However, I remained steadfast!

About a month after graduating from high school I used my savings and took a two-week vacation to the Dominican Republic. The beaches are to die for consisting of white sands resembling snow and the water a turquoise color that mystifies the senses. During my stay in the Dominican Republic I hiked, biked, kayaked and rode horses along the beach during sunset! What a breathtaking experience! My last day in the Dominican Republic I promised myself I would visit all the island nations in the Caribbean.

Two weeks after arriving from vacation, I landed a job at a local startup to write code. Although I was a green eighteen-year-old at the time I was willing to work hard! During the first three years working with the company my coding skills improved dramatically. In addition, I learned to work smarter and became a better communicator.

At age nineteen I moved into my own apartment. I learned early on how to budget my expenses such as rent payment, food, car insurance, utilities, and other stuff. Unfortunately, college does not teach students how to budget! When I entered my fifth year with the company, I was promoted to a junior leadership role as lead developer for the coding team. Little did I know at the time the so-called tech bubble was going to cause so much devastation in the tech industry seven months after my promotion!

Around July of 2000 we were told by upper management the tech industry was facing difficult times and drastic measures must be implemented to navigate the current economic turbulence. About eighty percent of my fellow employees, including myself, were given pink slips. My colleagues and I felt like we were hit by a thunderbolt! To add insult to injury my 401-k plan stock value was obliterated! Once my 401 k was worth three hundred thousand dollars and when I was laid off, I only had twenty-five thousand left in the account! I was completely crestfallen!

Even though I got burned in the stock market I had some money saved in my checking account, which was about fifteen thousand. Luckily, I had listened to my grandparents' advice to set some money aside for any of life's surprises. As time passed, I made an oath to never put all my money into a single investment! Three months after being fired, I would stare at the front wall in my room and be afraid to rise from my bed. In retrospect I was young and naïve and had not yet built the tough skin to handle difficult situations.

When I reached the fourth month of my unemployment journey, I decided to wake up early and take a one mile walk at the local park close to my apartment complex. Like anything in life, the first day to commence a new habit can be quite challenging! However, after a month of walking daily my mood and self-esteem improved considerably. I was feeling energized, and my go getter attitude returned once again! I started forwarding resumes, networking, and attending conferences with a positive attitude. Eight months later I found a job. Although I did not get paid great as before, still it was better than being unemployed. Many of my colleagues still had not found a job so I considered myself fortunate. For the next year, I worked for a local manufacturing company organizing their database systems, which were a mess!

While I was working with the manufacturing company, I found time to educate myself on financial and investments matters. Along the remarkable financial education journey, I learned about insurance, precious metals such as gold and silver, bond markets, real estate investment trusts, farmland, art, and other cool financial stuff too much to name that would pay huge dividends in my future!

As the seasons came and went my beautiful loving grandparents passed away because of ailments in the human body which form as we age. Even though I was spiritually and emotionally pulverized by my grandparent's death my faith helped me cope with their passing tremendously. I felt fortunate that my grandparents taught me humility, hard work, and to be prepared for the rough seas everyone encounters throughout one's lifetime.

The next few years I worked for a variety of IT companies and made lots of money. This time around I diversified my investments. I bought silver, platinum, and gold coins, which were so cool because I had never touched any precious metal in my entire life! I also bought a dilapidated duplex. My parents and a couple of friends helped renovate the duplex. On weekends instead of relaxing I would go early in the morning and work in the duplex. At first fixing a residence can be challenging, but over time I learned a lot by doing the work. Four months after purchasing the house I had tenants occupying the duplex and getting paid via rent. Over time I would pay off the bank loan by using the rent money and have a steady cash flow.

I felt better prepared this time to handle any unforeseen economic event that might rear its ugly head! Little did I know the Great Recession was going to throw the world into economic chaos and social upheaval last seen during the Great Depression! I remember during that time millions of people lost their homes, jobs, and stock markets around the world were decimated. To me it seemed that everyone got screwed except Wall Street and the banks!

Thankfully my mom and dad had retired a year before the Great Recession and had commenced new careers. The most important action that mom and dad had accomplished was to pay the house note. Regarding myself, I had developed four income sources outside my regular job to provide me an extra economic buffer. If I was to be laid off, I would already have a huge rainy-day fund to weather any economic storm. Like my grandparents used to say, all bad and good times eventually reach their finality! During the Great Recession I was still renting, which was an advantage at the time! By renting if I would lose my job, I have the flexibility to find work and move anywhere across the United States. Eight months into the recession most people and investors were avoiding stocks and real estate like a plague. However, I learned from reading many prestigious investors that the best time to buy assets is when everything seems to be falling apart. So, I started buying cheap stocks and acquiring properties at discounted rates.

The Federal Reserve was making it cheap to borrow money, so I jumped into the fire. In the fall of 2011 after much research, I purchased a thirty-unit apartment complex which had been foreclosed in Phoenix. I used a small amount of my money to purchase the apartment complex and the rest would be financed by a national bank.

Two months after doing repairs to the units, the apartment complex was filled with tenants and the money started flowing into my bank account, which is so cool!

For the next five years after the Great Recession, I managed to travel to all the Caribbean Island nations such as Turks and Caicos, Saint Barts, Dominica, Barbados, Jamaica, and the other beautiful island nations too much to name. I was fortunate that my parents and younger brother accompanied me to enjoy the enchanting Caribbean nations with their exotic foods, mystifying beaches, music, pristine wildlife, and of course the dancing.

By 2019 I had married the true love of my life James who currently is an independent registered investment advisor who has his own podcast and financial YouTube channel that teaches people about basic finance. James and I met at an investment conference in Charlotte. To make the story short we clicked, and the rest is history!

James and I purchased a beautiful home that is about thirty minutes from downtown Charlotte. The size of the lot is about an acre and a half. The house that we reside in is 3,300 square feet living area consisting of four bedrooms, two beautiful bathrooms, an office space for James and me, an entertainment center for family and close friends, a gorgeous kitchen and wine cellar. The backyard has a modern swimming pool design, a gazebo to engage in pleasant conversation and a custom-built sauna.

Everything changed dramatically in 2020. First like many people across the world I learned from various reports that a pandemic was forming in the city of Wuhan and causing great distress in China's healthcare system. By March of 2020 the Covid pandemic tentacles had spread around the globe causing, death, economic, and emotional devastation! There had not been a global pandemic

of this magnitude since the Spanish flu in 1918! The

United States and other world economies closed

about a month for the first time in human history!

Mass protests were occurring across the world due

to Covid lockdowns and draconian restrictions! The

covid pandemic times were difficult for many

people, including myself. Personally, I lost an aunt,

uncle, mother-in-law, and a very close friend. James

had lost his mother, and almost his father.

Thankfully James's father has recovered and lived

with us for five months to regain his full strength!

My parents and younger brother were spared this

evil disease!

In the early spring the government announced that

millions of renters were eligible to delay payments to

landlords because of the covid pandemic. Fortunately, by

the grace of God all my tenants are section eight housing

recipients, which meant that I was still receiving my money. Unfortunately for other landlords who had regular renters many ended up getting foreclosed by their lenders such as national and local banks. A friend of mine who had worked every day for three years to purchase a couple of rental properties, lost everything! Later, I learned that big investment companies bought the properties at discounted prices from small landlords who had their properties foreclosed! Tragic!

Well, 2020 came and went and in April and May 2021 the federal government started to distribute Covid vaccines to the elderly at nursing homes, community centers, hospitals, dialysis centers, and many more locations. Although James and I lost some money during this difficult period, thankfully we had other investments that performed quite well. In summation everyone should have at least a couple of income sources in addition to one's primary job just in case a natural disaster, stock market crash, layoff, and other unexpected crazy things occur out of the blue. If I had not planned for my retirement and executed a long-term strategy, I would most likely have been wiped out by the Covid pandemic! Thanks for reading my story. Love from Charlotte.

Thanks, Rebecca, for your lovely story. This story demonstrates that a person can recover from a brutal financial situation. None of us can predict future events, but all of us can take the necessary steps to plan for retirement!

Key concepts of retirement to remember.

1. The earlier one starts putting money aside for retirement, the greater chance one has of a decent retirement! Don't procrastinate, start to save for retirement as soon as possible! Time does not wait for anyone!

2. The power of compound interest over time can be one's best friend for retirement!

3. The days of working for an employer for forty years are over! Because of global competition and automation, one is lucky to be with a company for ten years!

4. To have a decent retirement one must have more than three income streams other than one's primary job. Remember a company has no loyalty to its employees, only to its shareholders to maximize value when a recession comes along! This means pink slips for employees!

5. Everyone must be willing to learn at least some basics of retirement planning. Remember at the end of the game it is each retiree who should care the most about his or her retirement money!

6. If one decides to choose a financial adviser or retirement specialist, make sure he or she

is working for one's best interest! Also be prepared to ask a variety of questions to the people who are going to help with one's retirement plan!

7. When starting a defined contribution plan such as a 401 k ask what type of fees are involved. Many people are unaware that 401 k charge fees. Some fees can take off as much as twenty percent from an individual whole retirement portfolio over a lengthy period. Ouch!

8. Building wealth takes time, consistency, and patience. Quick rich schemes rarely produce positive results!

Chapter 10

Life Insurance and Long-

Term Care Insurance

Life insurance is something most people dread to

discuss! The fact is people die daily. Although life

insurance has the notoriety for final expenses, life

insurance can be used for many functions when one is alive. For example, life insurance can be utilized to pay for college, start a business, income replacement for loss of salary, retirement, and many other practical functions too much to cover.

Another topic that people loathe to talk about in the insurance realm is long term care. For many people, long term care insurance is rarely discussed by families. Long term care for many not familiar with the term is when a person is unable to bathe, eat, cook, clean, or use the bathroom for oneself! Unlike auto and home insurance long term care insurance is rarely advertised, because it is an unprofitable product for most insurance companies. Due to the advancement of medicine, people are living longer, which increases the cost of long-term care! Most Americans are not aware that long term care costs are the biggest bankrupters of baby boomers, not medical expenses!!! Long term care averages about $7,000 per month in a nursing home facility in the United States. Of course, in some nursing care facilities in America, long term care costs can be much higher!!

Anyone can see the proliferation of apartments being constructed who cater to people over fifty-five and nursing homes across the United States. The demand for these types of facilities is going to be growing in the foreseeable future! Most Americans believe Medicare covers long term care, which Medicare does not cover any longer. Long term care if not addressed will be a crisis for boomers and their children. In this chapter I will provide stories regarding the importance of life and long-term care insurance.

Hello America, my name is Cindy Rodriguez. I was born and raised in Albuquerque, New Mexico. I came from a hard-working blue-collar family of four consisting of my dad, mother, younger brother, and myself filled with faith and lots of love. Dad worked as a welder for a steel company and mother stayed at home raising my younger brother Jason and me. Although mom was raising my brother and I she had her part time hair salon which included pedicures to make extra money. Mom was great in her craft and many customers adored her workmanship.

As the years passed, my brother and I grew up into smart, active, hardworking and independent teenagers. After school I worked at a grocery store as a clerk and my younger brother was a stocker at a local hardware store. My brother and I were permitted to work if both of us were on the honor roll!

At the young age of twenty-three years, I graduated from nursing school in New Mexico. My parents and brother were so proud of me. Personally, I felt happy and relieved to complete my nursing degree and having a good paying job lined up for a large hospital in Albuquerque.

For the next three years everything seemed to be doing well in my life. I was twenty-six at the time and felt wonderful! Youthful optimism! Unbeknownst to me at the time, tragedy was just around the corner. On a Saturday morning my mother called the hospital frantically wanting to speak with me. I was surprised because my mother had never called me during work. Just before I answered the phone, I felt a sense of dread engulf my entire body. Then I heard my mom's sobbing, painful voice telling me that my kid brother had died in a training accident as an active soldier for the US Marine Corps. When mom informed me of my brother's passing, I was in complete shock!

As soon as I finished my nursing shift, I immediately went to my parent's residence to console both.

All I can say is when one loses a loved one unexpectedly, it is a difficult experience!   Minutes turned into hours and hours into days till my parents and I learned what had happened to my beloved brother's untimely demise. The tragic incident took place during a training exercise where an equipment malfunction caused the helicopter engine to shut down. All four members in the helicopter, including my brother, perished.

I don't know how my parents and I made it through the funeral. The hardest realization my parents and I had to face was that we would never see or hear Jason's cheerful smile and inspiring voice again. Now looking back thirty years which have passed swiftly I still miss my baby brother!

A little over three years after my brother's death I became engaged to the love of my life Diego Saldana whom I met at a Saturday brunch for young professionals. At first, I was not going to the event because I was exhausted. During the previous week I had worked overtime because two of the nurses in my department were not able to work. Thankfully my good friend Athena convinced me to come. Diego and I had a great connection with one another and exchanged phone numbers. As time passed the relationship started to blossom. Six months later Diego proposed, and I accepted. Both of my parents were extremely happy for me and Diego.

About a month after the wedding engagement my mother and I went to Sunday mass. Dad did not want to go because he felt a little under the weather and told mom he wanted to finish a woodworking project for a customer. By this point in time dad had been retired for about a year, but he enjoyed being active in his workshop. Mother and I gave dad a kiss.

The Sunday service was very beautiful, consisting of hope and redemption. When the service came to its finale a couple of our lady friends from church, mom, and I went to lunch at a local Greek restaurant which has a mouth-watering cuisine. All four of us engaged in cheerful conversation while enjoying the food and each other's company. A couple of hours later we said farewell to our lady friends and were on our way home. Mom and I brought dad his favorite Greek dish. Both of us arrived at the house and immediately changed into more comfortable attire. I had placed dad's food inside the microwave so the food would be warm when he decided to eat the meal.

I went to dad's workshop which is behind the house to inform him his food was ready. As soon as I entered the workshop, I saw dad lying face down still. Instinctively my nursing training kicked in! Sadly, dad had been dead for at least an hour. Most likely dad had died from a heart attack. Tears started flowing out of my eyes. I kissed his beautiful face and hugged him so hard. My beautiful, kind, and loving dad had passed away. My soul felt utterly crushed! Just felt completely hopeless!

The funeral service took place a week and a half later. Fortunately, dad's entire funeral service had been paid for many years ago. When dad was young his mother had died unexpectedly without having any life insurance. The family pitched together money from friends and relatives to pay for the funeral. The experience shocked my dad immensely that he became a strong advocate of life insurance to deal with life's unexpected tragedies. As soon as my dad got employed, he bought life insurance for his dad and himself. Later he bought life insurance for my mom, brother and me.

I was so depressed that my soul was crushed in two! Lost my beloved brother and now my dad! Like dad used to say sometimes difficult situations tend to pile up without end! However, dad and mom raised a strong woman who would keep going forward for loved ones and having a positive outlook in life! In the following weeks and months, I become intensely focused on my job. Although I was working hard, I made time for mom, Diego, and a couple of close friends!

About three weeks before my wedding a young woman in her late twenties rang the bell on a beautiful Saturday morning. At the time I was cooking breakfast which consisted of an omelet mixed with onions, eggs, sausage, jalapeno peppers, wheat toast, and delectable coffee for mom and myself. Mom went to open the door and see who it was. The young woman who was dressed in professional attire introduced herself as an insurance agent who was door knocking around the neighborhood prospecting. Mom invited the young lady into the house. When I had finished preparing breakfast and setting up the table to consume the delicious and intoxicating meal, I informed mother that the meal was ready! I also invited the young lady to join us for breakfast.

For the next couple of hours, the three of us talked mostly about life insurance. The part that particularly interested me the most was long term care insurance. As a

medical professional I am aware that our physical and

mental abilities decline considerably as we age. The

insurance agent did an excellent job in explaining the

benefits of having long term care as less stress for taking

care of loved ones. Mom and I decided to purchase long

term care policies for the both of us which required signing

a lot of documents. Two months passed and the young

insurance lady whose name is Ariel Segovia called mom's

residence with good news that both of us were approved for

long term care. Both of us were ecstatic! Years later the

long-term care insurance would be a godsend.

The next twenty-five years passed rapidly. By this

time, I was fifty-five years old, happily married to Diego

for twenty-five years with two wonderful twin teenage sons

getting ready to graduate from high school and go to

university. Our family had moved from Albuquerque to

Dallas, Texas for better economic opportunities. Diego by

this time had started his own highway construction business which has been operating for fifteen years and doing quite well! Diego has many contracts with the state of Texas and Oklahoma for road projects. Regarding myself, I was working as a nurse manager for a large hospital chain. I could have retired but I wanted to fully maximize my retirement benefits.

By this time point in time my husband, kids, and I had a variety of life insurance policies used for retirement income accumulation, money for the kid's education, and of course final expenses. Thankfully, Diego and I took the initiative at a young age to purchase life insurance policies for ourselves and children.

Mother had moved with us and had her own apartment behind the house. Diego and I made sure we had a spacious backyard, so mom has her beautiful fruit and vegetable garden. Moms' apartment has two bedrooms, kitchen, and a specialized bathtub designed for her age. My parents house in New Mexico was sold due to the fact mom

was getting older. Diego and I promised Mom that she

would have her own space to do her own things and

hobbies. Also, mom wanted to be with her two grandkids.

When mom's residence was sold, the sale proceeds were

placed in an annuity to be utilized as retirement income for

herself.

The time finally came that mother had to use the

long-term care policy purchased over two decades ago,

which turned out to be God send from heaven. Mom was

diagnosed with early-stage Alzheimer's. Having planned

so many years in advance I can continue my career

peacefully knowing mom is being taken care of by trained

caregivers for certain hours each day, especially when

Diego and I are at work.

On a beautiful Sunday evening in the backyard my

husband Diego and I were sitting down inside the gazebo

enjoying a couple glasses of wine and engaging in pleasant

conversation. Out of nowhere Diego told me he had been thinking about purchasing a long-term care policy for himself, especially since mom started using the policy. Diego could not bear being a burden on myself and the two kids in the future. Jokingly he told me I must carry him like a baby around the house when he no longer recognizes who he is! I wished him good luck and both of us smiled.

Three months after the evening conversation on long term care Diego proudly presented me with his long-term care policy during dinner. I hugged and told him he had made a wise decision which would save money in the future and cause less psychological and financial burden on the family. I told him welcome to the long-term care club. He smiled and gave me a big kiss.

Thanks for the lovely story, Cindy. This story summarizes the importance of planning for the future. Many people believe one can apply and be accepted at any time for long term care insurance coverage, which is not the case. If an individual does not qualify health wise, he or she will be rejected! Also keep in mind as one ages life and long-term care premiums increase. The moral of the story is the sooner one purchases a long-term care policy, the more likely he or she will be accepted and cheaper the premium. The next story will cover the stress of not planning for long term care in advance.

Hello, my name is Marva Johnston from Oklahoma City, Oklahoma. I currently am president of a local credit union. In the following paragraphs I will describe the tragic tale of not having long term care insurance.

Dad and mom were fortunate to work their entire working years with the same company, which is a rarity these days. My siblings and I were raised in a typical middle-class family with all the love and material comforts. Currently my siblings are scattered across the United States. As the years came and went all the siblings went their separate paths seeking career opportunities. The only one who stayed in Oklahoma City was I. I graduated from

the University of Oklahoma with a degree in Finance and a

minor in economics. The first job straight out of college

was for a national bank as an assistant branch manager. Six

months later I became a branch manager!

Five years later I got married and had two girls. My

husband and I bought a beautiful house in the suburbs with

good schools and other amenities. By this time mom and

dad had retired from their respective companies.

Unfortunately, dad was not going to enjoy his retirement.

Two years later dad would succumb to prostate cancer. Dad

was one of those people who hated going to the doctor and

had not taken a physical in years. By the time dad decided

to go to the physician the cancer had spread throughout his

entire body. Just two months after dad's diagnosis he

passed away. Father's death was a horrific incident, but I

had to go forward for the sake of my family, even though

my soul was crushed inside! I was really worried about how mom would be affected by the loss of dad.

The following years passed rapidly in which mothers mental faculties declined substantially! By this time, I had taken charge in paying mom's monthly bills. Gregory, my husband, and I had discussed on many occasions that it would be a matter of time before mother was unable to take care of herself! Therefore, I proceeded to inform my siblings of mom's situation.

I bluntly told all my siblings that all of us had to come up with money to take care of our mother! Just like I expected my so-called siblings came up with moronic excuses not to help mother with adult care expenses. For example, my brother told me he had many expenses such as mortgage payments, car loan payments, and other expenses too much to name. I responded to my brother that I also had my share of expenses as well. The other two siblings were passive resistant. All I know is my siblings were dead to me! Going forward, I had to take immediate and drastic action for mom!

The next couple of months were one of the toughest times of my life. Navigating the intricacies of finding adult care for loved ones can be overwhelming. However, along the turbulent path of my adult care education odyssey, I became more enlightened! First, I learned mom could not qualify for any type of private long-term care insurance due to her health. So private long term care insurance had to be scratched from the list. As I became more educated on long term care issues, I was left with a couple of options.

The first option was to self-pay and place mom in a nursing home facility. All the good private nursing home care facilities in the area averaged about seven thousand dollars a month. The high cost would quickly drain the investments dad had left for mom. In addition, there was no way I was going to place my mom in a nursing home away from me and my kids. My mother gave her heart and soul to her family. Mom deserves better!

The second option was to put her on Medicaid. All my life I thought that Medicare covered long term care, but I was dead wrong! One day I was reading moms Medicare booklet which the government sends to Medicare recipients sixty-five and older on a yearly basis and it clearly states Medicare does not cover long term care in bold letters. I felt like I had been struck by lightning! To qualify for Medicaid all mom's assets had to be spent down.

As issues were getting a little complicated, I went to Becky, a financial advisor and insurance agent whose specialty is retirement planning. I had known Becky since college who had written two overfunded universal life policies for my husband and I to utilize later down the road for retirement income. In addition, Becky wrote life policies for the kids to help pay for college or start a business. My husband Gregory, who has been supportive throughout the ordeal, accompanied me to Becky's office on a Saturday morning. For the next three hours I provided Becky with financial statement information regarding my parents' investments and my mom's current health status. Becky informed Gregory and I that she would work on a plan to keep my mom from going to a nursing home.

For the next three weeks Becky and I communicated constantly on what would be the best avenue for mom. The time came for Becky to reveal her plan. Dad's 401 k which had grown constantly, especially in the last three years, was converted into a constant income stream called an annuity. The annuity would be used to fund mom's long-term care for mother. Mom and Dad's residence which had been paid off for some time was going to be converted into a rental property for funding long term care as well.

Thank goodness my husband and I have an extra bedroom in our home for mom. The next three months my husband and I adjusted the residence to accommodate mom's needs such as handrails. Although mom could not qualify for long term care, my husband and I managed to find people who would take care of mother during certain times of the day. The people chosen to take care of mom had experience taking care of elderly people.

Another month elapsed and mom moved in with my husband, daughters, and I. About three weeks later the whole family had adjusted to mom's presence and the caretakers. Both of my daughters became more comfortable and emotionally closer with their grandmother. My husband also developed a closeness to mom as well, which is a double bonus!

About four months after mom moved in with us, we went back to Becky to thank her, but also to get long term care insurance for my husband's parents and ourselves. My husband did not want to experience the same ordeal I faced with mother. Thank goodness my parents-in-law decided to purchase long term care to protect themselves and their family. If my parents in law had not wanted long term care insurance, my husband would have paid his parents policies for them!

Although my husband and I are still in our mid-forties, both of us reasoned the earlier we attain long term care insurance the more affordable the premium and less burden for our children in the future! For the most part it can be difficult for people to imagine that as time moves forward one's mental and physical faculties will eventually decline. By the time one needs assistance it is too late to apply for long-term care insurance. As my friend Becky says, Fortune rewards those who plan early and punishes procrastinators!

When two months had elapsed, Becky confirmed my parents-in-law and both of us are all approved for long term care insurance. I was ecstatic! I thanked Becky for all the work she did to help my family be in a better financial position for the future!!

Thanks, Marva, for the beautiful and heart-warming story. Although Marva had to go through difficult tribulations for her beloved mother, she managed to succeed. As the two previous stories have demonstrated, having life insurance and long-term care insurance can be a godsend for life unexpected turns. Key concepts of life and long-term care insurance to remember.

1. The earlier one gets life and long-term care, the easier one can health qualify, and the monthly premium is going to be more affordable.

2. Long term care is the biggest bankrupter of baby boomers due to the fact people are living longer!

3. Older people tend to assume their children have an obligation to take care of them in

their twilight years, but in many cases, children are unable to! Some children don't have the mental fortitude! Other children live in different areas due to the fact their jobs or careers are in certain states which makes it difficult to take care of their parents. Also, simply put some children do not care!

4. Life insurance is not only utilized for final expenses. Life insurance can be used for retirement income, paying for a child's college education or a down payment on a residence.

5. Life insurance can be used to transfer wealth from one generation to another. By transferring wealth through life insurance, it gives families a huge advantage financially and less stress regarding money!

6. About seventy percent of people sixty-five
    and older will need some type of long-term
    care as they age over time!

7. The issue of long-term care can be a
    difficult and traumatic issue to discuss
    between older children and aging parents!
    However, the sooner long-term care is
    discussed and planned, the less financial and
    emotional stress in the coming years for
    parents and their children!

Chapter 11

Precious Metals

Commercials abound that one must have a 401-k

plan to have a successful retirement. However sometimes

the stock markets can have abysmal years like during the

1930s, early 1980`s, tech bubble of 2000, financial crisis of

2008, and the pandemic of 2020. Rarely are precious

metals talked about in the mainstream media. To the

uninformed precious metals are things like gold, silver, and platinum. Gold and silver have been used as money for thousands of years across the world. Silver can be utilized for solar energy, medicine, jewelry, electronics, and many other everyday modern uses.

In the following couple of stories, I will provide how precious metals can be utilized as an emergency fund just in case some type of emergency pops out of nowhere.

Hi everyone, my name is Simon Nguyen. I was born in the beautiful city of Baton Rouge, Louisiana. My parents were originally from Vietnam but had to flee due to the horrific civil war. If my parents and grandparents had not fled Vietnam, they would have been killed by the Communists for owning and operating fifteen grocery stores. Fortunately, my family had accumulated gold over the years and were able to bribe the south Vietnamese government officials to leave the country immediately! When the United States Vietnam war was to reach its finale, the Vietnamese local currency was basically worthless!

I remember vividly as a child my parents emphasizing the importance of owning gold and silver. For the next three years my parents worked every day in a variety of jobs. Although my parents worked every day for years, both were proud of their adopted country, the United States.

As time passed quickly my parents had saved enough money to rent a single-family home in a lower middle-class neighborhood. My dad found a job as a machinist working for an oil and gas company that paid well. Dad would take overtime and save most of his money to buy a house for the family. Two years after much hard work, persistence, and sacrifice, my parents put down fifty percent on a mortgage in a middle-class neighborhood with great schools. A year later I was born in January and then two years later in July my younger brother was born.

The most important trait my brother and I learned at an early age was to work. By the age of four I was doing chores around the house such as making my bed and picking up toys. At fifteen, I already, knew how to cook a variety of Vietnamese dishes, learned the basics of repairing a car taught by my dad and other real-world stuff one does not learn in school. During the summers I would help mother with her dry-cleaning business. My parents and grandparents inculcated the importance of getting a great education to improve one's position in life. After graduating from high school, I attained a full ride scholarship to my local university, Louisiana State University (LSU).

The next three years were memorable because I made a couple of lifelong friends and connections. Even though focusing on my studies was my main priority I would have time to socialize with friends such as drinking a few beers at a pub or dancing salsa.

After completing my engineering studies at LSU, I started working for an oil conglomerate as a design and cost engineer. For the next four years I traveled at the company's expense all over the world to countries in South America, Europe, and Africa. Life was going well till the Great Recession hit the oil industry in 2008. Many people were let go across the energy sector including myself. Although disappointed about losing my job, I remained cautiously optimistic for the future.

My 401 k had taken a thirty five percent hit, but I had bought gold and silver over the years that made my current unemployment status bearable. Three months after losing my job, I took a trip across the entire United States which was very meditative. The variety of landscapes from beautiful mountain ranges, lush forests, deserts, and beautiful beaches inspired my young imagination at the time.

Arriving back in Baton Rouge from my cross-country adventure, I was determined to succeed! During the next six months a strict routine was established where I would arise early in the morning to exercise and then have a light breakfast. The rest of the day was filled with activities such as forwarding resumes via email, attending job fairs, and networking with associates to increase my hiring prospects. At seven in the evening, all my immediate family would sit together and have dinner. By nine thirty in the evening, everyone in my parents' house would be in bed. Unbeknownst at the time, the strict regimen kept me focused mentally and physically.

A week after my six-month regimen an Austin based natural gas company offered me a high paying sales marketing position due to my experience. To sweeten the marketing position, the company offered to pay my moving and rent costs for the first four months of employment. When two months had passed, I had deeply fallen in love with Austin's vibrant nightlife, can do spirit, its outdoor activities, and of course the majestic hill country. In hindsight the shale revolution boom was about to start, which would make lots of people wealthy. By 2011 the company was making a lot of money, and I was promoted to vice president of operations. At the end of 2013 my stock value had risen to six million!

In mid-2014 I bought a beautiful house with all the amenities, which is twenty minutes away from downtown Austin. Once in a blue moon, I would go to the hill country with my fiancée and enjoy drinking wine at the wineries. Although my financial assets were performing well, I was still stockpiling gold and silver just in case something bad happened! By early 2015 my stock net worth had ballooned to thirty million dollars. Even though I was doing well financially, deep inside my soul I felt something was missing.

In mid-June after consulting a couple of estate planners I submitted my resignation letter. The management team was stunned and tried to convince me to stay. I thanked management for having given me the opportunity to rise along the corporate ladder. Overall, I remained resolute with my decision to walk away from corporate management at least for a time.

Three months after resigning, I married the love of my life Janeth at the local Catholic Church. The wedding was beautiful, and many family members attended. For our honeymoon Janeth and I went to Hawaii where we had a wonderful time enjoying the people, natural landscape, and the magical beaches. For the next year I worked from my home office and was able to spend more time with my family. In addition, my grandparents lived with me and Janeth for six months. During the six months' stay my grandparents grew to love Austin's hills and surrounding towns. The younger brother and parents would also come once a month on the weekend. A year after leaving the company I evolved into a calmer and patient person who can appreciate the simple things in life.

By 2016 the price of natural gas had collapsed significantly, which led to many energy companies declaring bankruptcy. Even my previous company was not spared by the collapse of the natural gas market. Just before I resigned from the company the stock price was about $60.00 per share and by 2016 it had gone to $2.00 per share. Fortunately, by the grace of providence I left at the right time! Thanks so much for reading my story.

The next story also covers the topic of owning precious metals.

Hello, my name is George Reynolds. I was born in 1989 and raised in the beautiful city of Reno, Nevada. My parents came from Sacramento,

California for career opportunities. A few months before I was born dad was transferred to Reno to turnaround a struggling grocery chain. Dad had the notoriety of fixing struggling stores. Mother found a job in the Reno local school district. When I turned five, mom had saved enough money to start her car wash business. The next six years mom worked night and day to expand her business and fortunately managed to succeed.

At eight years old dad taught me the basics of playing cards. I would get bored and confused playing cards, however as time passed my card skills improved substantially. I would read books and articles on the tactics of playing card games absorbing everything!

High school passed rapidly. During my high school journey, I completed my college Advancement placement curriculum. A month after graduating from high school, I informed my parents that I was going to try my luck as a professional poker player. Both of my parents were disappointed but approved of my decision. Now I had to execute my plan.

So, for the next two years I was fine tuning my card skills in a small professional circuit learning the minute details of poker such as reading body language and psychology of players. In the meantime, my parents, like hundreds of millions around the world were going through the Great Recession tribulations. Nevada's housing market was pulverized, and unemployment was sky high! Fortunately, dad did not lose his job, but he lost most of his money in real estate investments. Dad had bought six residences, a year before the Recession brought most of the world economy to the ground. Moms' car wash business slowed a bit, but the business was still turning a profit.

By 2012 my mom and dad had lost the properties which had been foreclosed and bought by big investment companies. Mom had found a high paying job as a procurement director for the state government of Nevada to add extra income for the household. Mother's long-term goal was to build up her wealth and dad's. Father bought and stored more gold and silver coins to protect against rising prices in the future.

In regard to myself I had played in the world series of poker and won a substantial amount of money. Unlike typical kids in their mid-twenties who would spend a boatload of money on fancy cars, houses, and lavish clothes, I instead chose to own less material stuff. When I was playing cards at casinos or go out with friends I would wear jeans, a nice polo shirt, Chuck Taylor shoes, and my dark aviator sunglasses. My splurges are a SUV beamer and about three designer business suits. I was renting a high-rise apartment with a nice view of Las Vegas consisting of two bedrooms and a one huge bathroom with a shower and a jacuzzi, kitchen with countertops of fine marble, and a living room with an entertainment center.

The best part of where I live is that I'm just fifteen minutes'

away from my workplace, which is the casinos!

Regarding my investments, I bought gold, silver,

platinum coins, bitcoin, invested in rental units, wine, and

contemporary art. I just had very little in the stock market

because I had seen and known people who had lost their

hard-earned money in the wall street indexes! I was not

going to be a sucker! I learned about gold and silver from

my dad and older guys who play in the poker circuit.

Previously I had never heard of gold and silver in my life.

Can you imagine I had never touched a gold, silver, or

platinum coin for the first time till I was twenty-five years

old!

Six months before the pandemic I had done more

than I could ever imagine. I had traveled all over the world

to gambling Meccas such as Macau, China, beautiful

Monte Carlo, Singapore, and many places too much to

name. Also, I had been blessed and had taken my parents to

a variety of Pacific islands with beautiful beaches composed of white sand and enchanting turquoise water such as French Polynesia, Fiji, Malaysia, Maldives, and Hawaii.

All seemed well till 2020 started. At first, I did not pay too much attention to what was going on with Covid. Regretfully I thought in the beginning the mainstream media was exaggerating Covid to improve their tv ratings, thus profits. However, around March I realized Covid was for real. The casinos were completely shut down. Only necessary industries were opened such as grocery stores, hospitals, food preparation centers, and critical government offices. Many small businesses failed due to lockdown restrictions and people being afraid to go out and spend. I knew a married couple in their early sixties who committed suicide because they had lost all their life savings in the small restaurant specializing in Thai food that locals and tourists enjoyed!

In early April of 2020 two of the elder guys in my gambling circuit who had taught me tricks on poker and the importance of owning gold and silver passed away from covid. The sad part was their families, were not allowed to be with their loved ones in the final moments of life. After those incidents I was afraid for my parents' safety, especially dad who worked as the store manager and had constant contact with people daily. Although dad took the necessary precautions, he got infected in mid-July along with mom. I would bring my mom and dad groceries to their front door. Mom had symptoms but she recovered quicker than dad. Dad took some time to recover. Although dad did not have to go to the hospital, he had a persistent cough that did not go away for seven months!

By mid-2021 many Americans especially the elderly and critical workers were getting vaccinated first by the millions. As 2021 progressed more people of different age groups got vaccinated, and the economy slowly recovered. However, things like food, rent, and gas were getting more expensive. Fortunately, my investments had paid off and made rising prices less problematic. Finally, by 2021 I was back at my job gambling at the casinos and with a purpose to be even more focused on establishing stronger relationships with my family and close friends!

Key concepts of precious metals to remember.

1. Precious metals such as gold and silver have been utilized for thousands of years across the world as a means of exchange.

2. Gold and silver are utilized in a variety of industries such as clean energy, medicine, aerospace, electronics, automobiles, jewelry, and other industries too much to name.

3. Gold and silver help protect one's net worth from inflation, especially these days where food, energy, and rent is expensive!

4. If the energy grid was to become inoperable
    due to a terrorist attack or an economic
    collapse gold or silver coins --could be
    utilized to buy, food, medicine, fuel, and
    other essential things for survival.

5. History tells us that paper money over time
    tends to dramatically lose its purchasing
    power!

Chapter 12

Wills and Prenuptials

Having a prenuptial agreement discussion can be quite heated, especially when one has many financial and physical assets. Many years ago, most people would stay married for longer periods of time. Due to structural changes in the economy, divorce has become prevalent and accepted norm. On average first-time marriages tend to end up in divorce between thirty-five and fifty percent of the time. When people get married more than two times, divorce rates increase exponentially!

Divorce can happen at any age due to lack of communication, financial issues, substance abuse, loss of respect, infidelity, and other issues. With a growing divorce rate, more people are inclined to having prenuptial agreements, especially individuals with a lot of assets to protect! Although prenuptial agreements can be seen by some people as selfish, it is an alternative way for a married party to avoid divisive conflicts and exorbitant legal fees in case a marriage ends.

Wills are also a necessity to have in one's toolkit. Most people are not aware that wills have been used in society for thousands of years to inherit property when a loved one passes away. When wills are completed early, it is easier to disperse assets amongst family members and can avoid future conflict. In the following paragraphs the importance of having wills and prenuptial agreements will be covered through stories.

My name is Janice Stevenson. I was born in Bismarck, South Dakota and currently reside in the beautiful southern city of Savannah, Georgia. Currently I am a retired sixty-eight-year-old with two grown children and three adorable grandchildren. At four years old my parents, sister and I moved from Bismarck to the highflying city of Chicago. Dad got a great job as a vice president in the department of Public Works for the city of Chicago. My dad had served his country honorably during World War two in western Europe. Like many people who had served in the war dad used the Gi bill to complete his Bachelor of Science degree in Civil engineering from Georgia Tech.

As soon as we arrived in Chicago my mother enrolled my sister and I in a prestigious Catholic school. My sister and I did very well academically. I was in the soccer and debate team, which finished in first place during my high school senior season. Graduation and summer recess passed rapidly. I arrived at Notre Dame and moved into my dorm room, which was going to be home for the next four years.

When I started my freshman year at Notre Dame I was planning to major in English literature, however that changed when I took an introductory economics course. I instantly fell in love with economics, because of its mathematical analysis and various interesting topics. During my four-year journey at Notre Dame, I was involved in a variety of student organizations. I traveled all over Western Europe and fell in love with southern

Germany's magical castles, cuisine, and culture. The city of Munich captivated my imagination! Spain and Italy were also wonderful places with their beautiful landmarks, architecture, history, and food.

Like a dream, I graduated with a degree in economics and started working for a manufacturing company doing budget analysis back home in Chicago. Surprisingly I met my future husband at the company sponsored Christmas party. Matthew worked in the engineering department as the lead mechanical engineer designer for the company's products. Matthew approached me and we started having an interesting conversation which evolved into a first date. From the first date onwards love sparks ignited the both of us. Nine months later Matthew and I were married. Memories of my first and only marriage bring a sense of joy.

By the time Matthew and I were married he was working for a different manufacturing company with great compensation and benefits. Matthew and I agreed that for five years we would postpone having children to advance both of our careers. When the five years passed, I had my first child Brandon in January and a little over a year my beautiful daughter Sarah was born in December. The birth of my beautiful children was one of the happiest times of my life. For four years I focused on taking care of my two precious kids and husband by cooking healthily!

Regarding myself, I made sure to read the newspapers every day to keep abreast of current events. In addition to keeping myself mentally sharp I managed to stay in touch with former coworkers for any future references. After four years I was ready to work once again!

It took me about three months to find a good job. Fortunately, one of my good coworker friends had informed me there was an open position for a finance administrator at a public school district. A month later I was working for the school district. Unbeknownst to me at the time, I would work for the district for thirty-one years!

When the kids were in their teens every summer I would go with the kids, my husband and parents to Europe. Unfortunately, my husband's parents had passed away. My parents-in-law were wonderful people who spent time with the family. The kids would learn a lot about the places traveled during the summers, especially Italy and Spain captivated their attention. By the end of high school both the kids spoke Spanish and Italian fluently. In a moment my two children graduated from the University of Illinois. My son graduated with degrees in electrical and biomedical engineering, while my daughter completed her degree in civil engineering. A couple of months after graduation my son Brandon found a job at a large IT company in San Fransisco, while my daughter found a good paying job in Jacksonville.

Five years after my kids graduated from college, dad passed away due to heart disease. It was a tough couple of years for dad, but he was a strong man and managed to live for his family. The only good thing from dad's death is that he is not suffering any longer. A year after dad passed my sister's husband passed away from brain cancer. Seven months later my sister sold her house and moved with mom to Savannah, Georgia to escape Chicago's brutal frigid weather! My sister and I had decided to sell mom and dad's residence and place the money in an annuity. The annuity income would be utilized to help take care of mother.

A couple of years after mom moved to Georgia, I decided to retire from the school district. I had a great pension and had invested in a variety of investments such as real estate properties over the years with my husband.

A month after I retired my husband placed divorce documents on the table for me to sign. At first, I thought it was a joke, but after looking at my husband's eyes I knew he was serious. I was shocked by my husband unexpected brusque action! Both kids tried to convince Matthew to consider marriage counseling. However, Matthew had made his decision, and the divorce process went forward. Five months later our marriage came to its conclusion after forty years! Matthew kept most of the rental properties, while I kept our main residence which had been paid in full for years. Neither of us touched each other's retirement accounts!

In retrospect I was starting a new chapter of my life as a divorcee. So, after consulting with my kids and older sister I decided to sell the house in the Chicago suburbs and move to Savannah Georgia. A year later I had moved from Chicago to Savannah, Georgia. I had sold my residence for a nice profit and utilized the proceeds to purchase a townhome about two miles from where my sister and mom live.

Although I was devastated from the divorce, the emotional support of close friends, sister, mom, kids, and grandkids helped me keep moving forward in a positive way. My sister and I became involved in the Savanah community and forged new friendships. Later, I was told my ex-husband had married a woman thirty-two years younger than him. A couple years later Matthew's young wife left him for a younger man! Karma can be cruel!

Thanks, Janice, for sharing your wonderful story. Many people tend to think that mostly young people divorce due to youthful immaturity. However, one of the groups whose divorce rate has grown exponentially is people over the age of fifty! There are many reasons for this increase such as couples drifting apart emotionally, financial difficulties, and many problems too much to name. Now let us go to the next story which takes place in the south.

Hello Darlings. My name is Deborah. I am from the beautiful and romantic city of Charleston, South Carolina filled with an exciting nightlife, and beautiful architecture that bedazzles the mind. I was blessed with a comfortable upbringing as a child and adolescent. Dad was a hedge fund manager, while mom was a veterinarian and former beauty queen during her younger years. I inherited her beauty people say and her sparkling green eyes. My parents tried to put me in many beauty pageants, which I detested. By nature, I was a tomboy who preferred playing sports with the guys and girls, especially soccer.

Due to excellent grades and a high SAT score, I was admitted to Duke University. The four years at Duke were challenging, but very exciting. Duke is where I met my best friend Cassandra and future husband. Cassandra was my roommate for four years. As one can imagine we shared many ups and downs in our young lives, but both of us managed to persevere. Tests, boys, food, and difficult professors were our constant problems. I graduated with a degree in biomedical engineering and was accepted to medical school at Duke.

Cassandra graduated with a degree in chemical engineering and found a job in Houston.

I met my future husband Enzo, the first and only true love of my life at a Duke Basketball game. He accidentally spilled his beer on my shirt. Love can be strange! Like a gentleman he apologized and tried to clean my shirt. To make a long story short we both clicked, and Enzo asked for my phone number. When Cassandra and I arrived at our dorm we talked about how cute and handsome Enzo is. He is about six foot two with an athletic build with black hair and attractive light blue eyes. The relationship slowly started to develop and grow till he proposed to me during my final year in medical school. He flew all the way from Qatar where he was working as a project manager for a large US energy conglomerate.

I remember that night like it happened only a second ago. We had eaten at an upscale steakhouse restaurant filled with delicious meats and vegetables that intoxicate the senses in Durham, North Carolina. The red wine that my love and I drank was to die for! When Enzo and I had finished dinner both of us decided to take a nice walk in a well-lit public park. That night had a full moon with the night stars, a sparkling pearly white and a windy breeze. When Enzo and I reached the top of a wooden bridge right above a small pond he got on his knees and proposed to me.

Enzo presented me with a beautiful red encrusted gem ring. The gem sparkled so beautifully that I felt entranced by the ring and Enzo's handsome smile. For a moment I paused but knew I wanted to marry him so badly.   I then gathered my thoughts and told him the sweet and melodious response" Yes, I will marry you, my love!"

Enzo and I kissed for a long time. It was like the most beautiful kiss ever done in history! A couple of months later Enzo and I were happily married. All our family and friends attended the wedding. The food was composed of mouthwatering meats, vegetables, fine wine, and a delicious wedding cake composed of dark chocolate and almonds that mystifies the imagination! For our honeymoon Enzo and I went to beautiful Saint Barts, an island in the Caribbean, and enjoyed the magnificent crystal-clear sparkling water and smooth white sands which resembles winter snow!

Four years later I finished medical school and completed my specialization in pediatrics. By that time Enzo and I were living in Houston, Texas.

Although Enzo worked longer hours and acquired

increased responsibility, he was compensated with

wonderful benefits. Enzo and I purchased a home in

Houston Heights where we fell magically in love

with the neighborhood homes, beautiful gardens,

and eclectic shops!

Both of us decided to remodel a once

prominent house that had fallen into hard times.   A

year after thoughtful methodical planning, large

investment of money, and hard work the house

became magnificent once again! Once the

renovation of the house was completed, we invited

friends and family for a house party. Close friends

and family loved the décor, quality of materials, and

interior design of the house. The backyard garden

was also loved by the guests, which is filled with

beautiful red roses, eastern purple coneflowers, gulf coast penstemon, and other lovely flowers!

For the next three years after the house had been remodeled Enzo and I had been to a couple of safaris in Africa, which turned out to be a spectacular experience! We also travelled to Europe and visited all the major cities. My husband and I would drive on our own into rural areas to get to know the common people and culture. Driving around Europe with its variety of landscapes and weather was a fun experience to say the least. Everything seemed to be going well.

A week before Enzo's birthday I wanted to prepare a nice romantic candlelight dinner at home for him. The day of Enzo's birthday both of us kissed one another and were out the door. That day was very busy because it was the fall season, and many kids had colds. Fortunately, one of the nurses reminded me I had to leave early.

During the next hour I bought food, ingredients and a freshly baked cake for Enzo's birthday dinner later in the evening. When I arrived home, I was shocked to see Enzo's car parked in the driveway. I placed the cake and food inside the refrigerator and proceeded upstairs towards the master bedroom.

As soon as I opened the door, I saw my husband cheating with my best friend Cassandra. Instantly I felt rage, shock, betrayal engulf my entire body and soul! Looking back, I still don't know how I was able to keep my composure. Just thinking about that incident still makes me cringe and sad at the same time!

A year after the unpleasant encounter Enzo and I divorced. We divided everything in half including the much beloved house in the Heights that Enzo and I had worked so hard to remodel. The tragic part about the house was that we were planning to have a couple of kids to fill the residence with joy and laughter. The year of my divorce was the toughest time of my entire life. I had to contend not only with the divorce of the man I was supposed to live for the rest of my life, but also the betrayal of my best friend in the entire world!

Thankfully I had emotional support from my parents that gave me the strength to endure. Also, I focused on taking care of my young patients, which has given me purpose! Six years after my heart wrenching divorce, I have slowly climbed up spiritually from my emotional abyss and am ready for love, but with a prenuptial agreement in hand.

Thanks, Deborah, for your heartbreaking story. Although Deborah was in emotional darkness for a time, she managed to find light once again in her life. Now let's go to the next story.

Hello, my name is Antoine Johnson. I was born and raised in Richmond, Virginia. Currently I am a forty-five-year-old former NBA professional who played for eight years in the league. My family consisted of a mom, dad, two older sisters, myself and our little dog Pete. Unfortunately, my grandparents had been deceased for some time. As a young boy I recall my mom and dad worked hard to provide food, clothing, and a beautiful small home for their children. Mom worked for the state government of Virginia while father worked as an independent truck driver. Dad would drive across the country delivering goods so his family could live a comfortable life.

Dad started to teach me the fundamentals of basketball at the age of five and recognized quickly I had a natural talent for the game. Whenever dad had time from his busy working schedule, he would do drills in the backyard basketball court with me. Seasons came and went. During my middle school basketball years, I averaged twenty points a game as a point guard, but dad would let me know I could perform better.

In my freshman year in high school, I struggled but worked hard during the offseason and improved. By the end of my senior season in high school, I was averaging thirty points a game and the team had won the state title. I was recruited by top level basketball programs across the country and ended up playing for a prominent team in the Big East conference. Also, during my senior year, I met my high school sweetheart Jennifer who is very supportive.

At the beginning of my freshman year in college, I received the horrendous news from mom that dad had been diagnosed with stage three pancreatic cancer. When I received the news, I was in complete shock. For the next three months dad was getting chemo treatment for his cancer. Dad would call daily encouraging me to be positive and move forward. My freshman year I dedicated it to my dad by being recognized as freshman of the year and second team all-Big East conference.

During the summer before my sophomore year dad succumbed to pancreatic cancer. The only consolation my family and I had was that we were supportive of dad till his last breath on this earth! Therefore, none of us had any regrets, which made it easier to grieve! Dad's funeral was attended by our family, my girl Jennifer, close friends, former and current coaches and teammates.

My focus was to be the best player as humanely possible for dad's memory! When my sophomore year ended, our team reached the elite eight. I made All American second team in the entire country and Big East player of the year! My close-knit family and I were ecstatic and humbled by the recognition of my play! Three weeks after the NCAA tournament I decided to go into the NBA draft! Before plunging into the NBA draft, I had consulted my family, girlfriend, coaches, and agent.

The NBA draft finally arrived. I was a little nervous, but cautiously confident! Hearing my name chosen as the seventh pick, brought a sense of accomplishment and joy to my soul. My mother, sisters, fiancé, agent, and a couple of close friends were with me at the draft. I came to the podium to thank the commissioner and the team that invested in me. For the rest of the evening, I celebrated with my people and thought about how dad made all this possible by teaching me the fundamentals of basketball so many seasons ago.

Two weeks later I signed a three-year contract for ten million a year. The first year I was fortunate to have great coaches and seasoned veterans who taught me basketball at the professional level. I would play sporadically, for most of the season from the bench. However, in the last twenty games before the conclusion of the NBA regular season, my playing time increased because key veteran players were out due to injuries. This was an opportunity for me to display my basketball talent. During the last twenty games as a starter, I averaged eighteen points per game!

When the season ended, I took two weeks' vacation to rest my body and mind from the grueling season. Three weeks after coming back from vacation I married my high school sweetheart, Jennifer. The wedding ceremony and after party was a small and private engagement. Only close family members and friends were invited. Even though the wedding was small everyone had a wonderful time. Good food, wine, singing, and dancing filled the air.

Two years later I had become an all-star NBA player after much hard work, persistence, and discipline. Also, during this time, I was blessed with two male twins Dante and Leonardo. Lastly for my hard work the team rewarded me with a six-year contract with a substantial increase in salary!

Instead of investing my earnings wisely, I went on a crazy spending spree. Later as the seasons passed, I would regret my spending decisions! One example of my careless spending was when I purchased a ten thousand square foot mansion consisting of twelve rooms, four bathrooms, an entertainment center for family and friends, a custom-built indoor basketball and pool, a large study room for the kids and myself, wine cellar, a magnificent kitchen and a spacious living room. The mansion is located on a five-acre spread that is gated to provide privacy and a quiet environment!

My beloved team had made the playoffs for three consecutive years and was just two wins away from the NBA finals! It was one of the best times in my NBA professional career. Unbeknownst at the time, my beautiful life was about to change.

At the beginning of the regular season, I severely injured my right knee in a play and had to be carried out in a stretcher to a local hospital. The diagnosis was quite bad. I had to get surgery and miss the entire season to recuperate. So, for the next year I threw myself into physical therapy and building up my body. As time passed, I was able to play my first NBA game a year after my injury in mid-November. The first game of my return I scored fifteen points and had five assists in twenty-five minutes of playing time.

By the end of the regular season, I had regained all my playing ability and finished averaging twenty-four points per game. The tragic part about the season is the team did not win enough games to qualify for the playoffs, due mainly to countless injuries of key players! During the off season I worked hard to improve my game. As the hot summer days came and went rapidly my off-season training was going well till the fourth of July. I had invited friends and family for barbecue and drinks for the fourth!

That year the 4th of July fell on a Sunday, which was rainy and humid. My friends and I commenced early in the morning barbecuing the delicious meats for the early afternoon celebration filled with food, drink, pleasant conversation, and music. As the day progressed, I kept on drinking throughout the day. Around three in the afternoon I had the moronic idea of doing tricks with my speed motorcycle. Ten minutes into my routine I made a wrong move and crashed the motorcycle.

My wife, mother, and two boys were at the hospital with me. Tears of joy trickled down my face. Slowly I realized that I was at the hospital due to my foolish stupidity! The doctors bluntly gave me the good and bad news. The good news was that I would be able to walk and run again. Now the bad news was I would be out for the entire season!

Looking back at this incident I was a complete buffoon whose actions deeply disappointed my family, close friends, teammates, coaches, management, fans, and sponsors!   As the days and months passed in the blink of a moment, I worked daily to get myself healthy. It took me two full years to play an NBA game. Although I came back from a devastating self-inflicted injury, I had lost a certain amount of my explosiveness which had helped me score in the past! The next couple of months, I got better, adjusted my game, and picked certain moments to utilize my remaining athleticism.

During the offseason our owner sold the team to a hedge fund company. My teammates, coaches, and I were not surprised because the owner had recurring health issues in the past! Father time was catching up to the owner. I knew the new owners would make changes to the roster a year from now due to the team payroll being one of the highest in the NBA.

Unfortunately, I was traded midseason for two cheaper younger players to a non-contending team. I was angry at first, but at the end of the day basketball is a business. My family and I would miss the city and fans, but we had to keep moving forward!

Fortunately, I managed to play for two more years in the NBA and retired at the age of thirty. The main reason is that I was having recurring knee pain problems, especially in the last two years of my NBA career. My family, doctors, and I concurred that retiring would be the wisest choice for my future health.

For the next three years I went back to school and double majored in mathematics and physical education via online correspondence. Just before dad passed away, I promised him I would complete my education!

Everything was going well in my life, except my marriage! My wife and I were both drifting emotionally apart. Looking back, a major part of the strain was financial issues. I had repeatedly told my wife before retirement that both of us had to be more prudent with our spending because the large amount of money was not coming into our coffers again!

My wife and I went to counseling many times trying to salvage the marriage for the kids and ourselves, but to no avail. Life at home had become so unbearable that both of us were sleeping in different bedrooms! The kids could see the animosity and friction in the home by our body language. Over time I came to the realization the marriage was at an end!

On a beautiful Saturday morning I presented the divorce papers to my spouse! My wife got quite upset and told me she would take every single penny from me. I let my wife scream and blow her frustration. I just kept my composure and stayed silent till she finished her speech. In some situations, silence is the best move.

Divorce is a difficult process not only for the parties involved, but more so for the children. Everything was split in half except the overfunded life insurance and the residence. The mansion was put up for sale where my ex-wife would receive eighty five percent of the proceeds. By giving my wife the larger share of the property with market estimates of four million dollars, I did not have to pay alimony, only child support, till the kids reached the age of eighteen.

When the divorce reached its inevitable conclusion, I felt like a ton of concrete blocks had been taken off my back. With clearer hindsight my ex-wife and I married too young. Both of us just lacked the emotional maturity to evolve as time passed. After the divorce I wanted to start a new chapter in my life in another state that has mountains and some land. Fortunately, one of my past acquaintances knew a seasoned realtor. Four months later I moved to Washoe county in Nevada.

I got a wonderful deal on the property which consists of fifteen acres of land with a twenty-five hundred square foot residence that was well maintained by the previous owner who had unfortunately passed away due to a skiing accident. I only had to make minimal changes to the residence. In addition to the property, I have a glorious view of the Sierra Nevada mountains each morning, which is lovely!

Now I had to decide what I wanted to do with my life. One of my friends who lives in Reno had told me an opening for a basketball head coaching position was available at a local high school. I submitted my resume and credentials directly to the human resource team. After a couple of weeks had passed, the principal scheduled an interview for the following week. The interview went better than expected. Three days later I was hired as head coach of the basketball team.

I inherited a basketball team which had not been to the playoffs for fifteen years. For the next four years my coaching assistants and I built the team from the ground up by instilling in the kids' good fundamentals and discipline! By the end of my fourth year of coaching, the kids made it to the state semifinal! I was so proud of the kids, their families, and the community at large for the success. The proudest outcome for me was seeing the kids mature into hardworking and responsible young men!

Soon my coaching success started to spread across the state of Nevada and the country. I was offered lucrative pay and benefits from division one schools as an assistant or head coach. After much consideration I ended up signing with a small division one school in Nevada. Although the pay was lower, I wanted to be close to home.

Five years after taking the position as head coach, the team reached the Sweet Sixteen for the first time in history! As I was blossoming in my coaching career my two teenage kids decided they wanted to live with me permanently. The main reason for the kids wanting to live with me was due to my ex-wife's drinking problem, which was causing great emotional distress! My two boys were just tired of their mom's shenanigans and wanted stability in their lives!

Three months later my two boys were living with me permanently. Both my boys knew they had to do their daily chores around the house and to focus on academics! Mom was also going to live with us as well, due to the fact she was getting a little slower physically.

Fortunately, I had built a couple of apartments about fifty meters from the main residence to accommodate family and friends when they would come to visit me. Mom's apartment consists of two bedrooms, kitchen, washer and dryer and bathroom that has a shower and jacuzzi.

When mom's house was sold the proceeds went into

a safe investment where she would receive monthly

income for life!

By this point in my life, I had completed my

will and estate planning to ensure my family would

be taken care of if I was to pass away unexpectedly.

My investments had recovered substantially. The

major lesson learned in my life's Odyssey is there

are highs and lows, but one must continue moving

forward with a positive outlook and smile!

Thanks

Key concepts of wills and prenuptial agreements to

remember.

1. Wills are essential to avoid family discord in the

future and expensive attorney fees!

2. A court will not accept gossip, only a legal
    document to disperse assets!

3. Even if one has very few material possessions, it is
    wise to leave a will prepared for loved ones!

4. The sooner one completes a will, the better because
    anyone can pass away unexpectedly!

5. Prenuptial agreements can seem brusque at first, but
    it is a way to protect ones hard earned financial
    assets in an event of a divorce!

6. Divorce rates are increasing substantially for
    couples over fifty years old who have accumulated
    wealth over many years.

7. When one has a prenuptial agreement a divorce can
    proceed smoothly and quickly!